FLY LIKE A GIRL

ONE WOMAN'S DRAMATIC FIGHT IN
AFGHANISTAN AND ON THE HOME FRONT

MARY JENNINGS HEGAR

Philomel Books

PHILOMEL BOOKS
An imprint of Penguin Random House LLC, New York

First published in the United States of America by Philomel, an imprint of Penguin
Random House LLC, 2020.

This work is based on *Shoot Like a Girl: One Woman's Dramatic Fight in Afghanistan and on the
Home Front*, by Mary Jennings Hegar, copyright © 2017 by Mary Jennings Hegar,
published by Berkley, an imprint of Penguin Random House LLC.

Visit us online at penguinrandomhouse.com

Library of Congress Cataloging-in-Publication Data is available

Printed in the United States of America

ISBN 9780593117767

1 3 5 7 9 10 8 6 4 2

Edited by Jill Santopolo. Design by Lori Thorn.
Text set in Iowan Old Style.

To my soul mate and the love of my life, Brandon.
We've each had our disasters and triumphs,
and they've made us who we are today.
I wouldn't have it any other way.
I'm so happy I found you, and I can't wait to see what's next.
Thanks for killing all of my spiders
but still pretending I'm the brave one.
You're so much more than I deserve.

For Jude and Daniel . . .
I love you big as the sky, and all your little bones.
Mommy loves you all the way to the moon and back again.

AUTHOR'S NOTE

It has been incredibly difficult to recount some of the events in this book. Many of them are hard enough to talk about with a close friend, let alone write about for anyone and everyone to read. I'm putting it all out there for the world to see, and it's terrifying. But many people don't know what Air Force Rescue does or that the Air Force even has helicopters. Many people don't know about the enormous contribution of the Air National Guard. Many don't think that there are women serving in combat roles. Others think that the women who do serve in combat shrink in fear when the bullets fly. I know differently, and I wanted you to know, too.

That said, there are security concerns associated with sharing the real names of some individuals still serving. On a couple of occasions, there are some who are perhaps not painted in the best light. For these reasons, some of the names have been changed. The Department of Defense has redacted a few key names and words (covered in black throughout the book). None of the stories have been dramatized, all of the accounts have been scrutinized by the Department of Defense for classified information, and they are relayed here exactly as I remember them. Most of these stories have been vetted by others who were there to ensure accuracy, but people do tend to remember some of the details differently. There were heroic feats of valor and questionable decisions throughout, but for the most part, we all did the best we could with the information we had in the fog of war. Without Monday-morning quarterbacking, what follows is my best attempt to tell our story as seen through my eyes and validated by my comrades in arms.

Go as a pilgrim and seek out danger
far from the comfort
and the well-lit avenues of life.
Pit your every soul against the unknown
and seek stimulation in the comfort of the brave.
Experience cold, hunger, heat and thirst
and survive to see
another challenge
and another dawn.
Only then will you be at peace
with yourself
and be able to know and to say,
"I look down the farthest side of the mountain,
fulfilled and understanding all,
and truly content that
I lived a full life and one
that was my own choice."

—JAMES ELROY FLECKER,
FROM THE POEM PLAY *Hassan*

PROLOGUE

I glanced out the window at the dark shadows of sharks just under the surface of the sea. Shaking my head, I willed myself to focus on the task at hand as I continued running through the checklist: checking my equipment, reviewing where the emergency release was on the door, miming unbuckling the seat harness and unplugging my comm cord, checking to make sure that the tiny oxygen bottle on my vest was charged and on. The bottle would provide about thirty seconds of air if we found ourselves plummeting to the bottom of the ocean. I was well aware of what to expect if we should have to ditch, as I had attended the thorough "dunker" training in Alabama, where you were strapped into a mock helicopter, shaken, plummeted into a pool, and flipped upside down. But out here in the ocean, there were no instructors standing ready to save you if you went under. There were no sharks in dunker training.

My summer had been filled with exciting missions: putting out wildfires in California, marijuana eradication from the vast national forests out west, and deploying to Texas for hurricane support. But my least favorite kind of mission would be the grand finale to that exhausting summer: a long-range overwater rescue mission. A fisherman on a freighter way out in the middle of the Pacific had been injured, so my crew and I had been dispatched to go pick him up and bring him to safety.

Years earlier, during my first assignment in the Air Force, I remember clearly sitting in a movie theater watching *The Perfect Storm* when the film came out. I had cringed, barely able to watch, as the crew on the rescue helicopter realized they were unable to refuel off of their airborne tanker to make it to dry land. When they ditched into the ocean, I thought to myself, *Whew . . . I really want to be a pilot, but I'll never put myself in that situation. You'd have to be crazy to fly a helicopter out into the middle of the ocean!*

Yet eight years later, there I was. Flying the same exact helicopter I had seen in the movie, out over the open ocean, unable to refuel, and looking for a shark-free place to ditch. Just my luck.

———— ✦ ————

We launched out of San Diego in the morning, but we packed our night-vision goggles for the trip home. According to our mission-planning session the night before, we knew that we'd be hitting the tanker for the fourth time after nightfall. We packed some sandwiches and water for the trip, but I wondered if I'd even be able to eat, given the situation. Plus, I knew I'd need to nearly dehydrate myself to avoid having to tackle the complicated dance of trying to urinate in the helicopter. The

MJ on board.

guys just needed to keep an empty bottle handy, but for me there would be a bit more work involved.

The blanket of clouds overhead kept our altitude to a few hundred feet above water, but the weather report assured us that the ceiling would break up as we got farther from land, which was good news. Clear skies would ensure that we would be able to climb up to refuel off of the back of the C-130 that would be accompanying us.

As we went "feet wet," which means crossing the coastline for the open ocean and waving goodbye to land, we stepped through our appropriate checklists. These checklists were innocuous enough, but they only added to my anxiety.

For whatever reason, having to ditch into the ocean, *The*

Perfect Storm–style, represented my greatest fear of all of the possible contingencies we could face as a combat search-and-rescue platform, and it was a fear I had to overcome each and every time I went feet wet. Whether it was a training mission over a lake or a real-world water rescue, I always had to make myself take a deep breath as I stepped through the motions of the overwater checklist. I knew I wasn't alone in this fear, but the rest of my crew seemed much more unhappy about the four aerial refuels we had scheduled during this flight.

To tell you the truth, as nerve-racking as it could be, aerial refueling is my absolute favorite thing to do. The goal is to aim the tip of the refueling probe into the basket at the end of the C-130's hose. The probe is a metal tube that extends out from the right lower front of the aircraft, about eight feet past the edge of the rotor disk. The hose looks like a fireman's hose with a round metal cage about eighteen inches across that has a stabilizing sort of parachute attached around it.

When we practice refueling, we follow the same steps each and every time. First we hold a steady course while we talk to the C-130 on the radio. They would execute a rendezvous by slowing down and creeping up behind and above us. We would answer by increasing power to climb and speed up. This was usually relatively easy when we did it real world, as we'd be light due to being on empty. It was a little more difficult when we would practice it if we were already full of fuel. Practicing this "single engine" (meaning with the power limited, as if you had lost an engine) was also a lot of fun, though. You'd need the C-130 to fly beneath you instead of above, and you'd dive down to the hose, trying to aim your refueling probe directly into the basket on the hose. You'd only get one shot at this, because technically, in real-world situations, you wouldn't ever have the power to catch up and try again. One and done, basically, so you tried pretty hard not to miss.

On our flight that day out to the boat's location, we hit the tanker to refuel about three hours into the trip. Then three hours later I took the controls for the second rendezvous with the C-130. It can be physically and mentally taxing to constantly have to refuel the helicopter, so the pilots generally take turns. As I settled in with the controls, Finn, the other pilot, chatted with the tanker on the radio, and the Flight Engineer (or FE) called out that he had the C-130 in sight above and behind us.

"Start your climb," he said.

I gently pulled up on the collective, giving the aircraft more power, and dipped the nose slightly forward to maintain our speed. As per my usual habit, I took a deep breath and wiggled my fingers and toes to release any tension. I've always found that the worst thing you can do on a finesse maneuver like this is to grip the controls too tightly.

As I climbed, I glanced over and above my shoulder every few seconds until the C-130 came into view.

"Okay, he's coming up on your right," the FE called out, tracking the tanker in tenth-of-a-mile increments. "Half mile out . . . point four . . . point three . . . point two . . . You should see him."

I looked up through the greenhouse, our nickname for the window in the roof.

"Got him. Coming up and right," I announced, my eyes glued to the tanker.

I took the formation position behind and to the left of the bird, and they extended their hose. We ran the refueling checklist, and I maneuvered into position directly behind the basket. At this point, you are flying in a tight formation very close to the other aircraft, so close that we sometimes signal with lights or use hand signals to communicate from our windows to theirs. This is the moment when, as a pilot, you feel very much in control. But the crew members in the back of the plane, the so-called backenders, tend to get pretty quiet at this point in the maneuver.

I settled in behind the hose and took another deep breath, singing quietly to myself off intercom, as I always did before I started to make a run. Slowly increasing power and pushing the nose over slightly, I hit the basket dead center with enough force to connect; then I continued up and to the left until I was in the refuel position and the fuel started flowing.

"Damn, MJ. I never want to refuel with another pilot again," the Gunner said. I smiled a thank-you. It was always a relief to everyone when we got the refuel over with—we had another three hours of gas on board now and could relax for a bit.

Refueling was a harrowing experience for the crew members in the back, as they had no control over the sometimes-bumpy aircraft flailing about, trying to "plug" within two dozen or so feet from the tanker at about 120 miles per hour. Some pilots would try to force it, making jerky corrections at the last minute or overcorrecting. Singing quietly always kept me from overthinking things and putting too much pressure on myself. It worked like a charm every time.

Whenever we flew a rescue mission over open ocean, I'd be blown away when the boat we were looking for eventually materialized out of the vast blue expanse of the ocean. It took my breath away every time. Nothing but deep, dark ocean for hours upon hours, and then, suddenly, our target appeared out of nowhere. It somehow felt like dumb luck every time.

The C-130 we had refueled from was on scene to support us and was circling overhead. They had already dropped their pararescue jumpers—also known as PJs—who had to parachute down to the boat to stabilize the patient. We got on scene right after our sister ship had picked up the patient and two of the PJs. When they were clear, we hovered in close to the boat to pick up the remaining two PJs with our hoist for the long trip back to land.

Now all we had to do was fly home. With the end of this long mission in sight, we climbed up to execute our third refueling rendezvous. Out in the middle of the vast blue ocean, the sun was just starting to set. Pretty soon we'd be on night-vision goggles, which would make our fourth refueling a real challenge.

We executed the rendezvous and connected to the hose without a problem, but when we began the refuel checklist, the Flight Engineer noticed that the gas wasn't transferring. No big deal. That could be any one of a million different issues.

Finn, who was flying at the time, gently jiggled the controls, trying to get whatever valve was stuck to unstick. Nothing. I flipped some switches back and forth. Still nothing. Finn decided to disconnect and try again. Nada. We crossed over and tried the other hose. No gas. *Not good.*

We disconnected again, floated back to the observation position, and started to discuss our options. Finn ran through the checklists and some troubleshooting options with the FE, trying everything we could think of. Then we plugged again and still couldn't get any gas. As our fuel gauge ticked down closer to zero, the cold reality began to sink in. My greatest fear was materializing before me. We were going to have to ditch the bird in the middle of the freezing ocean just before nightfall.

I kept my toughest poker face on, but all I could think about was the helicopter that had ditched during *The Perfect Storm* and the brave men on board, not all of whom survived that mission. I listened wordlessly, desperately hoping we could find another solution.

Finn, who was a more senior pilot than I, started talking about our strategy. We would try to get back closer to the boat, and he would hover over the water while we all jumped out. Finn also thought he could possibly lower us to the ship if we had time. He would then offset away from us and put the helicopter down in the water before egressing and trying to escape the sinking aircraft by himself. I started thanking the universe that we had PJs on board. We all checked our equipment and looked around at each other uneasily.

"Okay, so that's the plan. Anyone have any better ideas before I brief the tanker on it?" Finn asked.

His question was met with silence for several seconds. None of us liked the plan, I can guarantee it, but we didn't have any better suggestions. We glanced around nervously at one another, all of us racking our brains for any other ideas that might not be by the book. Then the FE piped up.

"Hey, why don't you try going zero G for a sec? Maybe the gas we have left will hit the top of the tank and shake something loose."

We looked around. It sounded a little crazy, but might it work? At this point we were ready to try anything, absolutely anything, to avoid ditching out in the dark, cold abyss below us. We nodded at one another, and Finn started a sharp climb. At the crest, he dumped the collective to reduce power significantly and nosed the bird over. We all floated, held down only by our seat harnesses, as unsecured gear flew everywhere. The recovery at the bottom of the maneuver made the pit of my already uneasy stomach drop, but we leveled out without incident.

The extra time we had taken pulling this maneuver would definitely put us in a bind if we ended up having to ditch, but we knew it was at least worth a shot. It was time to hit the tanker one more time to see if it had worked. I think we were all holding our breath.

We hit the basket on the first try and climbed up to the refueling position. The C-130 was already aware of the issues we were having, due to our multiple plugs, so there were a lot of eager faces looking at us from the window of the cargo door. I flipped the switch to begin the fuel transfer, and we all stared at the gauge. A quiet moment ticked by: nothing. Then the needle quivered and started to move.

"Fuel flow established!" I exclaimed to huge cheers. I keyed the mic and relayed the good news to the tanker. I could hear the relief in their voices as they went from possibly being our overhead search support back to just being our tanker. I drew a shaky breath and started to laugh, listening to my crew doing the same.

Maintenance would never figure out what had happened, but I knew I had my FE to thank for keeping us out of the drink. His suggestion to try the unorthodox maneuver was due to his deep knowledge of the system, not because he had read the suggestion in some checklist. That mission wouldn't be the last time that a Flight Engineer's vast systems knowledge would likely save my life.

We hit the tanker for the fourth time on night-vision goggles without any issues, and the mood on board lightened. As we came in to land at the airfield in San Diego that night, the runway and taxiway lights beneath us made it seem as if we were descending down upon a blanket of stars. We were all aware of what had nearly happened, and the jokes we were throwing back and forth as we approached the airfield were tinged with an undercurrent of almost wild relief.

As we descended, my happiness began to dissipate.

Man, I needed to pee.

ONE

WHEN I LOOKED UP INTO the stands and saw my parents, my dad waved at me as if to say, *Only seventy-five more minutes, right?* I flicked a glance across the field at my teammates hammering our opponent at the far end. When you're the goalie on a top-ranked high school soccer team, you learn to expect not to see much action.

It was a beautiful autumn Texas day, and the sky overhead was a deep, dark blue. I heard a rumble in the distance, but there wasn't a cloud in the sky, so I knew it had to be one of the F-16s flying out from Bergstrom Air Force Base in Austin. I craned my neck upward to catch a glimpse of the gorgeous bird. There it was. My eyes traced its arcing path across the sky. It was so beautiful, I couldn't tear my eyes away . . . *THUMP.*

The ball bounced off of my forehead, and immediately, two important things happened: 1) I became the second-string goalie, and 2) I learned an important lesson about staying focused on the task at hand. It was important to have dreams, but if all you did was envy those who were living out your dreams, you would never manage to achieve them yourself. Dream big, then force yourself back down to earth to keep plugging away at the minutiae that will bring those dreams within reach.

After the game my dad ruffled my hair as we walked to the car.

"Don't sweat it, sweet pea," he said softly in his heavy Alabama drawl. "Least they didn't score on ya. You've already lettered in tennis anyway." His words were sweet as always, but they did little to assuage my humiliation.

———— ◆ ————

My dad stood only about five inches above my five-foot-four frame, but he was thick through the arms, chest, and stomach. His full head of salt-and-pepper hair was always combed back neatly, and he was rarely without a bushy mustache. He was sort of a George Clooney meets Burt Reynolds meets Foghorn Leghorn type, and I loved him with all of my heart. David wasn't my biological father, but he had raised me since I was about ten.

My "real" dad, an abusive, racist jerk, was long gone by then, thank goodness. After a terrifying marriage to my biological father, my mom had found her Prince Charming in a gassy cowboy who could laugh until his face was red and he couldn't breathe. My stepfather was the one who showed me what real love was. I wasn't his child, but he loved me just the same, not because he had to, but because he wanted to.

Everyone in my family knew my dream was to become a fighter pilot, which was something I'd been talking about ever since I was a little girl. I knew it the first time I saw *Star Wars*. I wanted to be Han Solo, flying the *Millennium Falcon* through an asteroid field. David, a Vietnam vet, taught me what it meant to serve my country, and he did not distinguish between men and women on that topic. He never once discouraged my ambitions by telling me girls couldn't fly jets in combat, even though at the time no woman had ever done so.

"Sweet pea, if you wanna do it, I'm sure you'll do it," he always told me. David taught me that the warrior spirit wasn't only for men. He never said it in so many words; he just treated me the same as his own son, my stepbrother, Jeremy. He never said that I was strong "for a girl" or the bravest "woman" he'd met. I was always just strong or brave to him. Becoming a pilot wouldn't be tough "for a woman." It would be a great challenge to undertake, and he'd be proud of me just for trying. That was David. He had my back, no matter what, until suddenly, he didn't anymore.

———— ✸ ————

My first memory, as a four-year-old little girl, was seeing my biological father push my mother through a plate-glass door. My ten-year-old sister, trying to protect our mother, hit him in the back to stop him from going after her, and I sat on the fireplace and watched helplessly as he chased her around the circular ground floor of our tiny two-story house in Fairfield, Connecticut.

Elaine darted under the archway to the dining room, around the table and chairs, and through the swinging door to the kitchen with him hot on her heels. She made it around at least once before he caught her by her hair. My father had my sister by the throat a foot off the ground against the wall in the dining room while my mother screamed that he was hurting her and to let her go. I hugged my legs tight, arms around my knees, with my eyes closed, trying as hard as I could to pretend this wasn't happening, that this wasn't my life.

I don't know if it was at that moment or sometime later, but I knew I would never—*ever*—find myself trapped like that again: weak, unable to protect those I love from evil. But that was definitely the moment I figured out what feeling I hate most in the world: fear.

My mother, Grace, grew up in Jacksonville, Florida, in an incredibly abusive home herself. I suppose that is why she put up with the treatment she received from my biological father for so long; she didn't know any different. She came to feel as if she deserved the abuse for some reason, and to this day she is always quick to believe the worst about herself.

At seventeen years old, my mother had hoped my father was rescuing her from her violent upbringing, but instead she found herself right back in the nightmare she was so familiar with. Her children were the only thing that made her happy, and my sister and I were the center of her world. Elaine and I were just over five years apart, but we grew up in two very different worlds. Despite our father's violent outbursts, Elaine was still a daddy's girl, whereas I was closer to my mom. This enormous difference in our personalities continues to drive a wedge between us to this day; our worldviews are completely different. I feel like I was the lucky one—I was seven years old (almost eight) by the time my mother finally got us out, but my sister was already thirteen.

I credit a lot of my life's success to my mother's courage in getting us away from my biological father. Honestly, though, it wasn't until he cheated on her and left her for a short time that my mother finally managed to escape the monster. And although I was only seven, she confided in me when my father had called her, trying to convince her to come back to him. He told her that he wanted her to bring my sister and me back to live with him so that we could all be together, that he would put blankets over our heads before shooting us with his shotgun and then would turn it on himself. We could finally be a happy family together, in heaven.

We got on a plane to Texas soon after that phone call. My teenage sister gave my mother a hard time about leaving all her friends, but if my mom had gone back to him, I wouldn't be the person I am today. More likely, I'd be dead or at least in jail for finally giving my father what he deserved. Every once in a while, when someone calls me brave, I think: *Hell, flying helicopters under fire in Afghanistan is nowhere near as scary as the thought of being that little girl again.*

Refueling.

———— • ————

By the time I got hit in the head with that soccer ball, I had already decided I would become a combat pilot. But at the age of sixteen, I had no idea how complicated the path I'd end up taking would be. I did know that if I wanted to achieve my goal, I had to be the cream of the crop, so I set out to be the absolute best at everything I did. Over the coming years I would end up playing tennis, soccer, volleyball, basketball, and track while also participating in cheerleading and marching band. The band at our high school was a pretty big deal, always competing for the top state honors, and despite that one low point as a soccer goalie, I always enjoyed competing—working hard and playing hard.

As it turned out, one of my most momentous decisions in

high school came early, at the beginning of my freshman year, when I decided to run for class president. After I won, I was thrilled to get the chance to develop a wonderful relationship with our class sponsor, a Navy man, Mr. Dewey.

Mr. Dewey was a big early supporter of my dreams, echoing the things my parents had always told me about my natural leadership abilities and my courage. He became my mentor and my guide throughout the rest of my high school years. When it came time to obtain letters of recommendation for college my senior fall, I naturally sought out Mr. Dewey. As a veteran, I knew he'd be proud of me for applying for an ROTC scholarship. I had never mentioned my dream of being a military pilot to him, and given his experience, I was looking forward to his insight.

A few days after I'd made the request, I stopped by his classroom to pick up the letter. Mr. Dewey, with his thinning, combed-over hair and a rotund belly, was sitting behind his desk, sealing an envelope, when I walked in.

"Hey, Mr. Dewey," I called out cheerfully.

No response.

He was usually so friendly and kind, but that day Mr. Dewey didn't even look up at me as he handed me that sealed envelope.

"Here. Good luck," he barked. Then he picked up his pen and started making notes on some papers in front of him. I was clearly being dismissed.

Something must be wrong with him, I thought. Perhaps someone in his family was sick?

"Um, thanks. I can't tell you how much I appreciate it . . ."
I almost asked him if he was okay, but when he abruptly turned
away from me, I decided he wanted to be alone. I hesitantly
left, concerned about whatever he must be going through.

As I walked down the empty hallway, between rows of
quiet lockers, I looked down at the envelope I held in my hand.
It was only then that I started becoming suspicious. *Why did
he choose to seal it, rather than let me read it?* I wondered. We had
always had such an open relationship. It seemed strange. I
studied the letter intently, trying to see if I could read any of
it through the envelope. I couldn't make out any actual words,
but I could tell that he had failed to sign the form that accom-
panied the letter. Since I knew I couldn't submit the letter
unsigned, I decided to take that as justification to open the
envelope.

What I found inside blew my mind. Mr. Dewey's recommendation was anything but. Instead it was a scathing description of my lack of leadership ability, discipline, and drive—the
exact opposite of what he had told me time and again over the
past few years.

Now, I've never been the type to burst into tears, but losing
my temper? That was something I often had trouble con-
trolling. I didn't even think twice about turning on my heel
and storming down the hall to his classroom to demand an
explanation of why he would lie about me on one of the most
important letters of my life.

Without a single thought about the potential backlash, I
threw open his door, startling him as he sat there, still grading

papers at his desk. The door slammed into the doorjamb as I burst into the room, holding up the opened letter.

"What the hell, Mr. Dewey?"

My fury immediately melted into despair when I saw the look in his eyes. Instead of the guilt or shame I expected, since he had just been caught doing something underhanded and dishonest, he was looking at me with utter disgust.

"Watch your language, young lady. How dare you open that!" he sneered at me. "What's the name of your recruiter? I'm going to call him and let him know what you've done."

"How dare I? Are you kidding me? Is this how you really feel about me?" I managed to sputter out, crushed by the betrayal.

His expression softened slightly, but the disdain remained.

"The Navy is no place for you, Mary. What are you trying to prove? This isn't a game. Defending our nation should be left to the strong, and it's no place for a woman," he said, shaking his head firmly. "You can still do great things. Maybe one day you'll be the CEO of your own company! Trust me. You'll thank me one day."

For once in my life, no witty retort rolled off my tongue. I was in shock. Years later I'd look back at this and see it for the example it was. Mr. Dewey was simply the first of many people I would soon meet, a faction of American citizens who truly believed they had to protect me (and protect our nation's military) from harm by denying me the opportunity to serve. At that moment, however, in my first-ever experience with discrimination, I was devastated. In disbelief, I quietly turned and left his classroom.

I had developed a strong relationship with my recruiter over the last year, as I'd been navigating the process of trying to join the Navy, so I immediately called him from a pay phone in the cafeteria. My hands were shaking as I dropped the change into the phone. Now that the anger had passed, I could feel my eyes begin to well up with unshed tears. I braced my fingers on the side of the phone, trying to hold my hand steady enough to dial his number.

When I related the story to him, he was silent. Then I heard him draw a slow breath.

"MJ, I'm going to be honest with you. You might as well get used to this," he said.

Mr. Dewey might be the first, he told me, but he would most certainly not be the last person to try to stop me.

I grew up that day. The path ahead of me wouldn't be an easy one.

Good. I never liked things easy.

———— • ————

Despite this speed bump, I was happy to be accepted into the University of Texas at Austin. Now that I was slightly jaded about the Navy after my experience with Mr. Dewey, I joined Air Force ROTC instead. It was so exciting to be in a group of 150 kids who were all just a little bit like me: We all got made fun of in high school for not smoking pot, we all secretly thought we were Maverick from *Top Gun*, and we all wanted to serve our country. I knew I had found my home.

While I attended regular classes just like all the other UT

Austin students, I was consumed with all things Air Force. In my biology class, I would write in tiny print in the corner of my notes the entire Code of Conduct. I can recite it word for word to this day:

Article I: I am an American, fighting in the forces which guard my country and our way of life. I am prepared to give my life in their defense.

Article II: I will never surrender of my own free will. If in command, I will never surrender the members of my command while they still have the means to resist.

Article III: If I am captured, I will continue to resist by all means available. I will make every effort to escape and aid others to escape. I will accept neither parole nor special favors from the enemy.

Article IV: If I become a prisoner of war, I will keep faith with my fellow prisoners. I will give no information or take part in any action which may be harmful to my comrades. If I am senior, I will take command. If not, I will obey the lawful orders of those appointed over me and will back them up in every way.

*Article V: When questioned, should I become
a prisoner of war, I am required to give name,
rank, service number, and date of birth. I will
evade answering further questions to the
utmost of my ability. I will make no oral or
written statements disloyal to my country
and its allies or harmful to their cause.*

*Article VI: I will never forget that I am an
American, fighting for freedom, responsible
for my actions, and dedicated to the princi-
ples which made my country free. I will trust
in my God and the United States of America.*

I quickly became an expert on everything that had to do with drill and ceremonies. The drum corps–like formations and marching was like a choreographed dance, one that reminded me of my experience with the marching band in high school. I loved being a part of something so much bigger than myself.

It was 1995, and although the wars in Afghanistan and Iraq were many years ahead, I was always mentally preparing for the eventuality that we'd be involved in another conflict. I knew that I wanted to be a pilot, and the most important thing to me was to live my life in a way that ensured I'd serve with honor. I wanted to make my parents proud of me, to save the person beside me if I could, and to make some sort of lasting impact on the world.

I immediately set my sights on pledging an ROTC organization called the Arnold Air Society (AAS), which was sort of like a military fraternity and clearly boasted the top cadets. Although there was only one other female in the group, I knew I could hack it. Between the hazing—which could get intense—and the endless grilling of the cadets on military general knowledge, completing the process was pretty overwhelming, and my GPA suffered for it. But surviving the eight-week pledge process and being welcomed into the AAS was my greatest accomplishment to date.

The semester I pledged AAS was the first time in my life I truly felt I'd proved to myself just how tough I could be. In the years to come, I'd face many challenges; that semester gave me the mentality that if I could survive those hellish months, I could make it through just about anything. After that, my second year of college was an absolute breeze.

———— ❋ ————

In the summer of 1997, after completing my sophomore year, I went off to field training, which was essentially boot camp for Air Force officer candidates. And yes, I know this is going to sound strange, but field training was pretty much my version of Disneyland.

Field training is similar to enlisted boot camp, but it is shorter and is more focused on leadership rather than the brutal breaking down and building up of troops like you see in the movies. This was a rite of passage and a requirement for all cadets after their second year. It was only offered in the summer, but I was more than happy to leave the sweltering Texas weather behind and head to New England.

In June of that year, I shipped off to Westover Air Force Base, Massachusetts. Upon arrival, the hundreds of cadets were split up into flights, and each flight had a couple dozen people assigned to them. We bunked in barracks that always had to be inspection ready, and we were woken up before dawn every day by reveille and the even louder Military Training Instructors (MTIs). There were plenty of tough moments in field training, but honestly, I think meals were the worst part for me. I'm a slow eater in general, so I had a harder time than others basically scraping my entire tray into my mouth in fewer than seven minutes. You also had to get at least a couple of glasses of water down in that time, and you weren't dismissed until the water was gone. At the end of each day, we were all utterly spent from being physically and mentally challenged every waking minute. So it was a sweet relief to fall into our rock-hard beds every night to the gentle, comforting sound of "Taps" playing in the background. For most people, this was torture. But some of us felt right at home.

Several days into the training, we were finally sent out on the obstacle course. I could barely contain my excitement—I'd been looking forward to this since our arrival. None of us knew what the course would look like before we arrived, but we probably all had pictured the worst. I was relieved to see that the first few obstacles were challenging but easy enough. We would have to low-crawl under barbed wire, jump over logs, and clamber up cargo nets. I was like a kid in a candy shop. Finally, I felt like I was in the real military.

I coasted through the first three obstacles, but then I was met with a surprise at the fourth. The obstacle looked like a huge ladder built by a drunken giant. The rungs were two-by-six pieces of wood nailed to telephone poles at slight angles. It looked intimidating but awesome, and I couldn't wait for my turn. But as we lined up in front of it, the drill instructors shocked us with the news that the women wouldn't have to complete this particular obstacle. I shook my head in fury and immediately stepped to the front of the line. There was no force on earth that could have stopped me from getting over that obstacle. I walked toward it, eyes narrowed, utterly focused.

It was easy at first—you just stood on one board, leaned your hips against another board, and reached up to grab the third. Pushing down with one hand on the board at your hip, you would haul yourself up by holding on to the high board while lifting your legs up to the hip-level board. As you neared the top, however, the boards started getting farther and farther apart. My five-foot-four frame wasn't ideal for the task, and by the time I got to the second-to-last board, I could no longer stand on one board and reach the last board at the top. I paused for a moment and thought. I'd have to jump, hoping I wouldn't miss grabbing on to that high board. It was the only way. So I jumped.

I didn't miss. I grabbed hold of the topmost board and used it to get my legs over the hip-height board. Finally I could pull myself over the top, swinging my leg up over the last board. Then I sat for just a moment to take in the view. It was beautiful. The thirty or so other cadets assigned to my flight were all going crazy twenty-five feet below me. The surprised drill instructor, ignoring the raucous cheers, was looking up at me as if to say, *What the f**k are you doing? Get the f**k down here!* I laughed and flipped over onto my stomach to start making my way back down to the bottom. The way down was still scary, since I was unable to feel the plank under my foot before having to commit to each drop, but I felt so amazing, I barely noticed.

On a high from the cheers, the adrenaline, and the satisfaction of shoving that "chivalry" back in my instructor's face, I faced down the next obstacle. Piece of cake. It was a large log, about two feet wide and horizontal, held up at both ends by wooden braces leveled at about shoulder height. To "set up" the obstacle, the instructors would roll the log a few inches toward the cadet. This way, when the cadet would run at, jump on, and swing their leg up over the log, the log would begin rolling away from the cadet, so we could roll with the log to the other side. I volunteered to go first again, eager to keep my awesome streak alive. Running full steam ahead, I hit the log and threw my leg up. However, the instructor hadn't reset the obstacle, so instead of rolling with me, the log had rolled toward me.

The smack of my knee on the log sounded like a mallet tenderizing a steak. The next smack was my back hitting the ground. I looked up at the beautiful sky, the same one I'd been enjoying from on high a moment ago, and an intense pain exploded up my leg and into my back. It was clear to everyone that I was badly hurt. I was instantly surrounded by my flight as the drill instructor pushed his way through the crowd to get to me. Then he called for assistance on his radio. My baggy cargo pants started to feel tight.

The instructor, noticing the swelling, pulled a pocketknife out and cut my uniform right above my knee and gasped audibly. He keyed his mic again and upgraded his request to an ambulance. He began to gently unlace my boot, but the pain was intolerable, so he just cut the laces and removed my boot. As the paramedics loaded me into the ambulance, my instructor climbed in next to me. He knelt beside me and held my hand as the driver bumped along the uneven ground. I gritted my teeth, willing myself not to cry.

I was in warrior mode, refusing to shed a tear, but then everything around me started to sort of sparkle. Darkness was creeping in at the edges, my vision shrinking to an ever-smaller ring. The drill instructor began smacking the back of my hand, trying to get me to talk.

"Hey . . . HEY. What's your name? Where are you from?"

I felt like I was going to puke, but I managed to bark out, "Cadet Jennings, Austin, Texas, Drill Sergeant!"

He chuckled. "You can turn it off, Jennings. You're going to be fine, but stay with me. You want to be a pilot, right?"

I was shocked. How did he know that? I guess pretty much all of us did.

"Yes . . . why?"

"You do know that if you ever pass out and that gets on your record, you can't fly, right? So if you're hurting, just f**king scream and cry already. It's better than going unconscious."

It turns out that the collision between the log and my knee had succeeded in cracking my kneecap completely through. Luckily, it was still in one piece. You can't cast a broken joint, though, so I was just told to stay off of it. My mom and dad, who were picking me up from the airport, held hands and watched with pitying eyes as I was wheeled over to them in a wheelchair by the airline attendant. I had gone off to show everyone just how tough I was, but I couldn't even return home under my own power.

I couldn't have known it then, but I would end up returning to officer training the following year and graduating in the top 10 percent of my class. However, I'd have to complete the training with a knee injury that would plague me for the rest of my life.

As I rolled down the airport walkway to the baggage claim in a wheelchair, my dad ruffled my hair. "Aww, come on, sweet pea. Don't look so sad. You're not invincible, ya know. We still love you, darlin'."

My trademark hormonal teenage bad attitude always came out at the worst moments. Instead of letting myself be consoled, I refused to meet his eyes. "A lot of good that'll do me," I growled.

For some reason I still can't quite understand, I was always pretty brutal to my stepfather. David was absolutely wonderful, and I did love him with all of my heart, but I made it a point to never admit that to him. Maybe I just wasn't ready to trust another father figure.

As I grew older and realized I *did* want to tell him that I loved him, it had been built up so much that I wanted to wait for some kind of memorable occasion. I pictured him giving me away at my wedding, and before we walked down the aisle I'd turn to him, kiss his cheek, and finally tell him I loved him. I pictured this scene more often than I care to admit.

But later that fall, I'd have my last chance—and I'd miss it. On the night of October 5, 1997, I was at my parents' house doing laundry and mooching dinner like any good college student. It was my junior year in college, and by then I had mostly recovered from the broken kneecap. My knee would never be the same, but I was no longer in a lot of pain.

After dinner I helped clean up the kitchen, and we all started winding down for the night. Then David told me he had a gift for me, that I'd be getting my Christmas present early this year, which was very uncharacteristic of him. He handed me a box with a huge smile on his face, and I flopped on the couch, rolling my eyes at his enthusiasm, to open it up. It was a cell phone! In the late nineties, this was a huge deal—I couldn't believe it.

"Now, if *that* doesn't get me a hug, nothing will!" David said, holding out his arms for a hug, thrilled by my excited reaction. But I didn't even look up from my new phone.

Instead, I walked right around him and into my room, already programming in all of my phone numbers, wanting only to play with my new toy.

"I love you, sweet pea," he called out after me.

"Yeah, I know. Thanks," I said.

That was the last time I ever saw him alive.

David went off to work the next morning, forty-nine years old, full of life, and happily married. I woke up a bit later and drove into Austin to go to my nine A.M. class. At around ten A.M. I received a phone call from a hysterical secretary at my mom's office. She was screaming that David was dead, that my mom was having some sort of breakdown. I guess the secretary didn't realize that she wasn't just talking about my mom's husband. She was also telling me that my father was dead.

"Wait . . . what did you say?" I must have repeated the question about five times. I understood that my mom needed me, but my brain refused to register any other information. The secretary told me my mother was huddled under her desk, screaming and crying, and no one could get near her. I got in my car and drove like it was the end of the world, running red lights and using the emergency lane on the highway.

To be honest, I don't remember what happened when I got there. Instead of being helpful, I entered into a sort of a zombie-like state of numbness and disconnection. I don't even really remember leaving her office that day. I do know that I didn't cry. I didn't make eye contact or talk to anyone. I drove to the airport to pick up incoming relatives who would pretend to care, but I said almost nothing. I was stone-faced; no one could tell that I was barely hanging on to my sanity.

David worked for Praxair, a natural gas company. His co-workers told us that he had been checking the level of one of the tanks with a flashlight tied to a long rope. We were told that the standard procedure was to lower the flashlight into the tank in order to ascertain the level of the liquid by measuring the rope. Apparently, he had slipped on the ladder, either on his way up or on his way down. The flashlight's lanyard got wrapped around his neck somehow, and he had accidentally hung himself. As soon as his coworkers had found him, they cut him down and administered CPR, but it was too late. And while we all had our theories as to how he fell, we would never know exactly what happened. The only thing I knew for sure was that the world had become an ugly, unfair place very quickly.

Suddenly, I found myself unable to trust any kind of happiness. It was too fleeting, completely temporary. It would be almost fifteen years before I'd let myself be truly happy again.

I've been in love with the same poem, "High Flight" by John Gillespie Magee Jr., since I was a child. It had always represented the joys of flight to me, and I'd kept it pinned up in my room for many years. But after David's accident, it would forever bring to mind thoughts of my dad and my hopes that he was in a better place.

> Oh! I have slipped the surly bonds of Earth
> And danced the skies on laughter-silvered wings;

Sunward I've climbed, and joined the tumbling mirth

Of sun-split clouds,—and done a hundred things

You have not dreamed of—wheeled and soared and swung

High in the sunlit silence. Hov'ring there,

I've chased the shouting winds along, and flung

My eager craft through footless halls of air.

Up, up the long, delirious, burning blue

I've topped the wind-swept heights with easy grace

Where never lark or even eagle flew—

And, while with silent, lifting mind I've trod

The high, untrespassed sanctity of space,

Put out my hand, and touched the face of God.

———— • ————

After David died there was nothing anyone could do to break through to me. At that point I had dropped out of my classes and moved home to help my mom, but I don't think I was much help to anyone. The two years I had left in college loomed large before me, and I was trying hard to remember why I should keep pressing on toward my goal when life would just rip anything I obtained away from me and replace it with pain. Then, just two weeks after David died, in the midst of my pity party, I got a phone call. A friend of a friend, not knowing about my tragedy, called to tell me that she had found out about a White German Shepherd at a nearby shelter. She knew I had been looking for one for months and was excited to let me know there was one nearby. I immediately dropped everything to head out to the shelter to meet the dog.

When I arrived, they shook their heads and apologized to me, telling me that I'd wasted my time making the trip. They informed me in no uncertain terms that he was "not adoptable" and that I should look elsewhere. This dog was aggressive and heartworm positive, but I begged them to let me meet him anyway, and in a rush, I told the clerk about my dad. The news about this dog, I told him, trying not to cry, was the first thing that had cheered me up since his death. Out of sympathy, the man handed me some dog food to give him through the fence to help me make friends. He walked with me down the wet cement hallway to show me where the dog's cage was located.

"He's the seventh down this row on the right. Don't get too attached, though. He'll be put down tomorrow."

As I walked down the row, the dogs started barking. I ignored the chaos and kept walking, but when I reached the seventh gate and looked in, I didn't see a White German Shepherd. I saw a brown dog, all jutting ribs and sad eyes, with a broken and floppy left ear. It was the only dog not barking. He didn't even look at me. That was okay—I knew exactly how he felt.

I sat down next to his cage and started talking to him, but the dog still wouldn't budge from the back of his kennel. The other dogs had settled down by now, but still, the dog wouldn't move. On a whim (and because I really didn't care if I got hurt), I opened the gate and climbed inside the cage with him. The kennel was just a patch of cement floor about three feet wide and twelve feet deep, surrounded by a chain-link fence.

I decided to get comfortable, bracing my back against the fence on one side and putting my feet up on the other side. It looked like getting to know each other might take a while. I tossed some food toward the dog, but he wasn't interested. So I leaned my head back against the fence and started telling him all about my dad. About how much I adored him and how angry I was at God for taking him from me, especially when terrible people like my biological father still breathed air.

"I don't even think there is a God," I told the dog. I hung my head and finally, finally, the tears I'd been holding back ever since I got the news about David started to flow. As I cried and cried, the dog finally stirred in the back of the kennel. Inching toward me, he started eating the food I had offered him. Eventually, he came close enough to start eating it straight out of my hand.

Just then all the other dogs started barking again, loudly. The dog grew visibly agitated and began shaking. A little nervous, I made eye contact with him for the first time. The yelping of the frenzied dogs reached a crescendo, and the German Shepherd lunged at me. I gasped and covered my face, bracing for the worst, but all I felt was his fur on the back of my hand.

I opened my eyes and saw that this beautiful, dirty, weak dog had protectively placed his front paws on my right side and his back paws on my left. He was standing guard. The dog was shaking and ready, poised to kill anyone who would try to hurt me.

I reached out my hand to pet him, and he flinched at my touch but didn't pull away. I ran my hand along his side and

Jäger.

could see the white hair beneath the layer of dirt and grime. It made me wonder if I was also still there, somewhere beneath all this misery. I began crying again, knowing I had found my dog. The clerk, whose appearance had caused all the barking, had come out to check on me. When he arrived at our cage, he was shocked at what he saw. He opened the gate and helped me up, cautiously eyeing the growling shepherd. As the door latched behind me, I caught the clerk's eye.

"You're not killing my dog," I told him in a firm voice. "What do I need to pay, and where do I need to sign?"

I named him Jäger (pronounced like Chuck Yeager). *Jäger* is the German word for fighter pilot, hunter, and rifleman. I had fallen in love and found my dog, but the next six weeks were incredibly painful for both of us. Jäger had to undergo heartworm treatment, which is basically the equivalent of getting dosed daily with arsenic. I visited him each day and just sat and cuddled with him as he recovered.

Jäger slowly regained his health, and in that time, he became my constant companion. I would spend the next eight years covered in white hair, but I wouldn't trade one moment with him for anything. I had met my canine soul mate.

Jäger helped me find my way back into the world, helped me trust that good things could happen to good people. I went back to school with him at my side, believing once again that I could decide my own future. David wouldn't have wanted me to give up on my dreams after his accident. Now Jäger was helping make me mentally strong enough to start chasing my dream again.

I would return to field training the next summer, and it would feel very different from the first time around. It was like the sharpness of color had been drained out of the world, and I experienced everything at a lower volume. Without the excitement of learning all I could from the training, I struggled to enjoy the experience. Each night that summer as I drifted off to sleep, I would listen to "Taps" play on the loudspeakers over the camp. It was no longer a comfort to me, and the lyrics now never failed to make me cry.

Day is done, gone the sun,
From the lakes, from the hills, from the sky;
All is well, safely rest.
God is nigh.

TWO

THE FOLLOWING SEMESTER I was ready to go back to school, but I'd decided to commute from my mom's home rather than moving back to campus. Jäger had restored me emotionally enough to face the outside world, but I was a different person when I rejoined my fellow ROTC cadets. That next year, my junior year, was filled with mistakes. I took crazy risks, either out of a determination to kill myself or a sense that nothing I did mattered.

At a convention in New Orleans, I was goofing around with some fellow cadets and jumped from one balcony to another on the thirtieth floor of a hotel. I nearly fell and carried a softball-sized bruise on my left biceps from where my arm caught the railing. I bought a sport bike and drove it like it was stolen all over Austin. Some nights I would take part in illegal racing at a closed-down airport. A few months into my return to school, I even threw out my plan to wait to have sex until I was married. I fell in love with a cadet named Jack, although in hindsight it wasn't really love. It was more like I was trying desperately to run from myself, to stanch my emotional bleeding, to numb the pain of losing my dad.

I was still with Jack during my senior year, and as school started winding to a close, the pressure on the ROTC candidates only increased. The way the selection for pilot training works is as follows: Each cadet is scored on various aspects (class ranking, GPA, physical fitness, etc.) throughout their time in the Corps (the Reserve Officers' Training Corps, or the Corps of Cadets). The seniors' scores are stacked against other ROTC senior cadets throughout the country in different universities, all of whom are "categorizing" in their second-to-last semester. The Air Force takes however many people they need for pilot training, and the rest of the cadets have to pick a different field, such as Intelligence, Security Forces, Aircraft Maintenance, and so on. Contrary to popular belief, only about 20 percent of the officers in the Air Force get to be pilots.

Throughout ROTC, I had consistently been getting around 425 or so out of 500 on the physical fitness test. I could max the upper-body-strength stuff like push-ups, but I could never max out the points for the sprint. When the day finally came for us to do our categorization physical fitness test, or PFT—in other words, the only PFT that counted toward getting accepted into pilot training—I injured my knee on the sprint and logged the worst PFT score of my career: somewhere around 280. I was incredibly disappointed, but given the fact that I was in the top of my class (I was serving as the second-in-command at the time, the Vice Wing Commander, as chosen by our cadet Wing Commander), I thought I still had a chance.

I was wrong.

When the results came out, I found myself standing on the sidelines as the names of those selected for pilot training were called out. They would come forward to receive giant silver-painted cardboard wings around their necks. I found myself trying to smile, taking pictures of my friends and acting as if my world hadn't just come to an end—again. I was excited for them, so I had to paint a smile on my face for the day. Behind the smiles, I was devastated, of course, but I was already hatching a plan for my next step.

Some people who were disappointed that day resigned from ROTC to pursue their plan B, but I wasn't going to let this knock me off my chosen path.

Though I had failed to get a pilot slot out of ROTC, I knew there were other roads that would lead me to pilot training. However, I also knew that it was incredibly difficult to travel those roads, as the majority of pilot slots go to the ROTC and Air Force Academy graduates who "win" a spot during categorization. For the rest of us, the fifty-thousand-plus people who composed the rest of the Air Force officers, there were a couple of pilot slots a year offered as a carrot, but only the absolute best of the best would ever grab that extremely rare golden ring.

I was faced with the decision of whether to find another dream or to join the military in a different career field and hope I could rise to the top. I decided to roll the dice and risk it. I looked at the list of career fields before me. Which one would make me a better pilot someday? I chose Aircraft Maintenance, as it would afford me the opportunity to learn about aircraft systems. I figured when I finally got to pilot training (not *if*, but *when*), I'd be ahead of my peers because of my experience working with different airframes.

I was ecstatic when I was selected. After I completed my training, my first assignment would be heading off to Japan to work on F-16s. I couldn't imagine a better assignment. The only problem was that I was planning to marry Jack, and he still had a year left at UT.

This assignment to Japan seemed perfect to me in every way, except for the fact that it meant my soon-to-be husband and I would be spending the first year of our marriage on separate continents. *But,* I thought, *we were in love. Love can overcome anything, right?* So we got married as soon as I graduated, and I accepted my commission into the US Air Force. We had a midsize ceremony, and I wore the big white ball gown and everything. That should have been my first red flag that I was doing something completely contrary to who I really was. Jack and I took a honeymoon cruise in the Caribbean, and then off I went alone into the wild blue yonder at the age of twenty-three, starting my dream career. Not flying planes— not just yet—but in my head I was practically already in the pilot seat.

———— • ————

In January of 2000, I reported to Aircraft Maintenance Officers' training at Sheppard Air Force Base in Wichita Falls, Texas. I was a newlywed and a green, eager, young second lieutenant in the Air Force. My plan was simple—I would learn all I could and rise so far above my peers that the Air Force would have no choice but to send me to pilot training.

My class was made up of a dozen or so officers just like me. We were all fresh from our commissioning sources, which varied from ROTC to the Air Force Academy. None of us was quite sure what to make of the new "butter bars" on our shoulders—so named for the golden bar that looks like a slice of butter—that identified us as second lieutenants. We were all hoping we had made the right decision as we embarked on the beginning of our adult lives.

On the first day of class I walked into the building, nervous but excited. Strolling down the hallway looking for the classroom, I felt like it was my first day of high school all over again. I knew I was in for a long three months of learning the basics of aircraft maintenance management alongside people I'd never met. I'm an introvert, always have been, and I'm never very comfortable in a room full of loud strangers. I took a seat as close to the back corner as I could and sat quietly, absorbing all the noise around me. I took a deep breath and reminded myself that I'd only have a couple more months in a classroom, and by April I'd be actually doing my job stationed at my first base in northern Japan.

As I sat there listening to the other officers chatter around me, I noticed that there was one voice that was consistently rising above the rest. I quickly pegged the loudmouth jerk in the front row as someone I planned to stay well clear of. He was a rough-and-tumble kind of guy, with a shaved head that showed off the many big scars he appeared to be proud of. I'd learn later that they were from a mix of bar fights and hockey games. Raised with mostly brothers in the wild Alaskan tundra, Keenan Zerkel was a tall, dark, muscular, handsome pain in my ass. His deep brown eyes were never without some sort of mischief, and if he was talking, you can bet he was offending someone. We had a connection from our very first meeting— we hated each other. It seemed like I couldn't even raise my hand before he was retorting with some sort of smart-ass comment. And I couldn't seem to help myself either—I returned the favor as often as I could.

Our class instructor seemed to share my opinion of our class troublemaker from the very first day. Over the next few weeks Captain Randall was constantly sparring with Keenan, trying to assert his authority. But Keenan apparently had it coded into his DNA to fight all forms of authority, so Randall's attempts to control him seemed to only make it worse. I found out later that Keenan had almost been kicked out of the Air Force Academy right before graduation for breaking curfew and raising hell. Looking back on what I know of him now, I have no doubt he would have ended up killed in a brawl or thrown in jail if not for the Air Force. Getting into and graduating from the Academy likely saved Keenan's life.

Keenan's hopes of becoming an Air Force pilot were born from his time flying Cessnas and seaplanes in the wide, blue skies of Alaska. Despite our instant mutual dislike, we recognized the same stalled dream in each other. So despite my greatest efforts to avoid him, I couldn't help but relate to him. Near the end of our three months of training, Captain Randall walked into the classroom in the middle of one of our famous arguments.

"Whatever you say, babe," Keenan goaded. He never missed a chance to call me "babe" or "honey" in a dismissive way. By that time I guess Captain Randall had had enough, because he pounced.

"Lieutenant Zerkel!"

"I told you . . . Call me Zerk," Keenan drawled lazily, drawing chuckles from our classmates.

Captain Randall was not amused.

"Lieutenant, that's sexual harassment, and I'm not warning you again. Meet me in my office after class."

When Keenan arrived in his office that afternoon, the captain handed him a Letter of Reprimand. The LOR was a serious thing, and it meant that Keenan's entire career would be kicked off with something negative being added to his file. When he told the class what happened, we all sort of laughed.

"That'll teach you to disrespect me," I said with a wink.

"Oh, so you need him to fight your battles?" Keenan joked.

I punched him in the arm.

"Ouch! That's assault! You should get an LOR," he retorted sarcastically.

When the three months of training ended, we all went our separate ways. The Air Force's newest Aircraft Maintenance officers scattered to the four corners of the world. Some of the officers were sent back to the United States, some were sent to Europe, and Keenan had, coincidentally, been assigned to the Pacific Air Forces (PACAF), just like me, for our first assignment.

The course had prepared us with knowledge of logistics, supply chain issues, tool and equipment control, aircraft forms, systems, and any other information we could learn from a book. Now, 99 percent of our learning would happen on the job, in the hands of the experienced senior noncommissioned officers assigned to our flights.

None of us had any true intentions to stay in touch, but I think we all hoped we'd bump into one another out in the "real" Air Force in the coming months and years. Sure enough, not long after training ended, I was surprised to receive a phone call from Keenan, whom I hadn't spoken to since we'd left Texas. I was immediately suspicious, wondering what he wanted from me. Apparently, Captain Randall had put what he saw as sexual harassment into Keenan's permanent record. And while I was amused, I knew he didn't deserve to have it impact his career.

Keenan might have been a loudmouth, but my classmates and I all knew he would make a very good pilot. Under the asshole facade, there was a solid, loyal, brave man with unwavering integrity and a passion for flying as strong as my own. I would have trusted him to watch my back over any other person I knew in the Air Force, and that's saying something. If I ever found myself in a bar fight, I'd hope to see

Keenan Zerkel's face. Then again, if Keenan were there during a bar fight, it probably would be him who started it in the first place.

I asked Keenan what I could do to help, and he asked if I would write him a supportive letter. Of course I would, I told him, and I'd also help him track down the rest of our classmates. We rallied behind him and told Captain Randall's boss how we felt. It was practically unheard of, but we successfully got the report pulled from Keenan's record.

Strangely, this mini battle we fought against the bureaucracy brought us closer as friends. We got the derogatory report rescinded, and a mutual respect formed between us. Since he had been assigned to a position in Korea, while I would be in Japan, we kept in touch pretty easily. Our training together was over, but it certainly wouldn't be the last I'd see of Keenan Zerkel.

In early April I boarded the long flight to Japan, excited to get started with my life as an adult, though I was a little apprehensive as to what this new chapter would have in store for me. I was married, but I was separated from my husband by oceans and continents. I was working toward my dream, but I was also working in a career field that was highly male-dominated and filled with people who treated me as if I didn't belong. Most of them seemed to assume I'd be bad at my job, until I proved them wrong, so I found myself starting over and establishing credibility every time I joined a new team, which at this stage in my career was about every six months.

At least I had my best friend, Jäger, with me in a kennel in the cargo hold of the plane. The vet had given me a mild sedative that would make him sleep for most of the trip, and he eagerly ate up the "magic hot dog" I spiked for him before takeoff. We had to spend the night in the Tokyo airport, and I hated having to keep him in the kennel. I slept with my fingers through the grate, gently caressing his fur. He had an all-pink nose—which is rare for a Shepherd, as they're usually black—that I affectionately called his little piggy snout. It was so adorable to see him sleep cozily in his crate with his head resting on his little stuffed piggy dog toy. I woke up to the sounds of Japanese people *ooh*ing and *aah*ing about him, asking if they could take a picture with the gentle giant I had in a cage. Apparently, dogs his size were quite rare in Japan.

My husband, who was still a cadet finishing up his last year at UT, had a nonexistent paycheck, so I would be paying both my bills in Japan and my husband's bills in Austin with my tiny paycheck. That winter was tough—there were times when I couldn't even afford to turn on my heater, so I spent many nights that year sitting up in bed, reading aircraft systems manuals, wearing two pairs of sweats and socks. At least I wasn't too lonely—I could always snuggle up to a big, fluffy Jäger to stay warm.

My first assignment at the base in Japan was to lead a flight of backshop maintainers. The Air Force groups its personnel into various levels of organization, and the smallest group is called a flight. Usually the biggest group on a base is the wing. Each wing is divided into groups, groups into squadrons, and finally squadrons are split into flights. Depending on the amount of work a flight must accomplish, it can range in size from a dozen or so to a couple hundred people.

The backshop is where the behind-the-scenes maintenance is done when aircraft and/or equipment is taken off of the flightline. The majority of aircraft maintenance happens in the backshop flights (like Fuels, Engines, Avionics, etc.), but the fast-paced action happens on the flightline. The "flightline" refers to the taxiway, aircraft hangars and parking, and the buildings housing the flightline maintainers and pilots. Most, if not all, new officers are broken in running a backshop flight before they are sent out to the flightline.

Those who work on the flightline live and die by the flying schedule. Working the flightline meant turning aircraft quickly, getting them ready to fly, and making sure they were safe. It often required fourteen-hour shifts in the freezing, horizontally blowing snow. I would have to spend six months paying my dues in the backshop before I would earn a place on the flightline. And although I know it doesn't sound tempting, the flightline was exactly where I wanted to be—in the middle of the action, learning and being challenged every day.

During my first week in Japan, when I reported in to my first commander, Major Johnson, I did all of the things my college ROTC instructors had told me to do. I ironed my service blues, which resembled a not very flattering blue polyester business suit. I proudly placed my "training" ribbon, which showed that my training was complete, on my jacket across from my name tag, shined my shoes, and pinned my hair up nice and tight. I reported to his office and sat ramrod straight in a chair outside his door, waiting patiently to be called in.

"Jennings . . . get in here," I heard him call out from inside the office.

I stiffly marched through the doorway and stopped two feet from his desk. Popping a sharp salute, I could barely contain my smile. I was excited to be starting my career and meeting my first commander, to begin a mentoring relationship I was sure would span the next twenty years. I couldn't wait to learn all he had to show me.

Major Johnson's office was dark, musky, and smelled of cigars. Even when he was seated at his desk, he was still an imposing figure with a brusque demeanor. He stood well over six feet tall and reminded me of Bigfoot, only without all the hair. His high-and-tight military haircut revealed an enormous head, one that matched his burly frame.

"Sir, Lieutenant Jennings reports as ordered!" I was to hold my salute until it was returned, as I had been taught. With my eyes focused at an imaginary point in front of me, I could see Major Johnson eyeing me up and down, taking in my strict adherence to military decorum.

"S**t," he said under his breath. "Lieutenant, the first time your time of the month gets in the way of doing your job, you're fired. Now get out of my office."

He didn't return my salute. He just glanced back at his computer, ignoring me, not saying another word. I stood there frozen, still saluting, shocked into silence by what he had just said. Then, contrary to all of my training, I slowly lowered my salute and did an about-face. The fact that, in his mind, I didn't even rate a returned salute did not bode well for my time assigned to his squadron. I was at a loss for why he would show such a lack of respect for me after having just met me. As I walked out of his office, I tried to think of all of the possible reasons for the interaction. Was I being tested? Should I stand up to him?

I decided to give it a few days so I could get a bead on him. Sure enough, it was just as I feared. There was no underlying lesson to be learned. He was just a misogynistic jerk. I'd have to keep my head up, toughen up, and learn to get along with someone who clearly disrespected everything I was trying to accomplish. This wasn't the first time I had to bite my tongue, and it certainly wouldn't be the last. To be honest, I would learn a lot from my short time working for him because, after all, you can learn a hell of a lot from the leaders you do *not* want to emulate.

———— ⬥ ————

I feel strongly that your success in life has little to do with your situation and everything to do with your reaction to it. Instead of wallowing in despair, I chose to funnel the frustration I was feeling at moments like this into being better at absolutely everything I did. One of my favorite places to do this was at the range.

We had to qualify to carry various service weapons, which

involved simply stepping up to the target and firing your weapon. Depending on how many shots you got in the center, you either fail to qualify, qualify, or shoot expert. Throughout my career, whenever I hit the gun range to qualify, I would always leave with an expert rating. Whether I was using a handgun or a rifle—no matter what—shooting always seemed to come naturally to me.

After the incident in Major Johnson's office, I got the chance to blow off some steam at the range in Misawa. Once again, I qualified expert, and one of the instructors there high-fived me to congratulate me on my shooting.

"Outstanding, Jennings. You shoot like a girl."

I stood there baffled. Did he just compliment me or insult me? Was I going to have to deal with this kind of s**t here, too?

Seeing my expression, he quickly elaborated. And what he said would stick with me for the rest of my career, every time I picked up a weapon.

"No, really," he continued. "Women are physiologically predisposed to being excellent marksmen. It's about their muscle tone, center of gravity, flexibility, heart rate, respiration, and, in my opinion, psychology."

"Really?" I responded, fascinated by this news.

"Yes, seriously," he went on. "You see, there's a lot of ego involved in how well you shoot. Frame of mind is one of the keys to accuracy when firing your weapon. If you put too much pressure on yourself, your grip tightens and you sabotage yourself. A lot of guys let their egos get the best of them and feel like they're not a real man if they can't shoot. The chicks come in here and have fun. I try to teach my guys to shoot like a girl when I can. You know, the Soviets were extremely successful at using women as snipers during World War II."

He smiled once again, then turned away, leaving me standing there in silence. There were physical advantages to being a woman in combat? I went home that night and did some more research. Turns out he was right. I learned that women in general even handled G's better than most men. "Pulling G's" refers to the acceleration vector downward when fighter pilots execute sharp turns or climbs. It's that feeling you get in the pit of your stomach at the bottom of a roller coaster when all of your weight seems to multiply and you feel like you're being pressed down into your seat. In people with more upper-body strength, pulling G's sends blood away from the brain, which can result in "G-LOC" or G-induced loss of consciousness. In those who have more lower-body and abdominal strength (like most women), it's easier to execute the maneuver that prevents G-LOC. This is done by tightening your legs and stomach, thus preventing excessive blood from flowing away from your brain and pooling into your legs.

If this was true, and the military seemed to make decisions about who should do which job based on gender stereotypes, why not make all of their snipers and fighter pilots women? A long shot, sure, but the research helped me see how equally absurd it was to bar women from certain jobs without even assessing them individually to see if they had the right stuff.

I was proud of myself for shooting like a girl, damn it, and I planned to fly like a girl one day soon. I'd be the best pilot in the Air Force.

———— • ————

After those six months behind the scenes in the backshop under Major Johnson, I was sent out to work on the flightline, where the tempo was a lot faster and the hours were longer. I didn't mind working my tail off, but it did make it difficult to find time to work out. I fought against my old knee injury to go for a run now and then, but usually I spent my free time exhausted and home with Jäger.

The flightline is where I finally *did* find a leader worth following, but in an odd twist typical of the confusing military hierarchy, technically, I outranked him. Senior Master Sergeant (SMSgt) Matt McCabe was the senior noncommissioned officer (SNCO) assigned to my flight and, as such, he was the highest-ranking enlisted member under my command. Air Force officers tended to move around throughout their career in order to get a good breadth of experience, but the SNCOs and other enlisted members usually stayed put for longer to develop a greater depth and expertise in a specific field. Sergeant McCabe had been there for a few years, and he would prove to be a gold mine of information and leadership lessons for me during my time with him.

I don't know how he did it, but he was the most squared-away airman I would ever meet. His uniform was always clean and crisp. Somehow, at the end of a fourteen-hour shift during an exercise wearing chemical gear and gas masks, he still managed to look like he had just gotten out of the shower. He took great pride in the fact that he ran a tight ship, and by the time I took the reins, his flight was already producing excellent results.

One day, early on in my time on the flightline, I was addressing the group of mechanics under my command. Sergeant McCabe stood next to me, towering over me with his hands on his hips. To this day I don't remember what I had been saying, but he nodded in approval as I laid out the law to my flight. He then walked back toward my office with me, asking me if I had a minute to chat. I was about to make an excuse that I was too busy when he grabbed me by my upper arm and pushed me through the door to my office. "No. We need to talk now."

Shutting the door behind him, he proceeded to lay into me about leadership, telling me in no uncertain terms why what I had just said to my flight was the complete opposite of what I should be doing. I was shocked. "Why didn't you say anything out there?" I asked him.

"Because that would undermine your authority. I'm not going to let them see me be disrespectful to you . . . I'll agree with you in public, but in the future maybe ask me for my opinion in private before f**king up the flight I've been building for months."

Officers would come and go from the flight, but Senior Master Sergeant McCabe would be there to stay for a few years until his next assignment. It would be the last time I made the mistake of overlooking the true leader of the flight and disregarding the greatest resource I had at my disposal—his years of experience and his willingness to teach me rather than oppose me.

They say that for every terrible officer out there, there's an SNCO who failed the Air Force. Well, Senior Master Sergeant McCabe took his job of turning me into a good officer very seriously, and to this day I remember him as one of the greatest mentors I had in the military.

———— ❖ ————

Now that I was all settled into my new job in Japan, it was time to start preparing to apply for a pilot slot off of active duty. In order to even be considered, I needed the endorsement of my entire chain of command and, basically, to be rated the number-one choice from the whole base. I had to do everything I could to make myself competitive.

In August of 2001, I went back to the States for a couple of months on temporary duty at Kirtland Air Force Base in Albuquerque, New Mexico. I had requested and been granted a slot to attend the Aircraft Mishap Investigation School, which would, I hoped, make me look even better on paper to the higher-ups. The optional course was only about six weeks long, but it would make me an enormous asset to the base should there be any type of incident.

On September 11, 2001, a few weeks into the program, I woke up and began getting dressed for class as usual. The news was always on in the background, but what I heard that morning froze me in my tracks. Someone had crashed a plane into one of the World Trade Center towers, and smoke was rising from the skyscraper like a chimney. I was glued to the television as the reporters speculated as to what had happened. Mechanical failure? Air traffic control error? I was sure whatever it was, we'd be discussing it in class.

As I stood to turn it off, I watched in horror as the second plane impacted the tower on live TV. This was no accident. My stomach turned as I began to realize that we were under attack. Kirtland was on lockdown as I drove in to class that day, and Humvees with mounted weapons made their rounds. Flight schools across the country were closed. Air traffic was closed to nonmilitary flights for a short time. Our country would never be the same.

Unfortunately, in this most unstable of environments, I had already made plans to obtain my private pilot's license. The first step in pilot training during these years was supposed to be in the T-3 aircraft, but the fleet was grounded for some mechanical issues. As crazy as it sounds, sending pilot candidates to get their private licenses became the Band-Aid solution until another suitable resolution could be arranged. Now that I was back in the United States, I wanted to take the opportunity to achieve this critical milestone, and I was willing to use up all of my leave to do so. I decided to spend the entirety of my leave hanging out with my family and my husband in Austin while going to school for a few weeks to learn to fly. Getting my license on my own, I knew, would make me a much more attractive candidate; it was one fewer step that the Air

Force would have to pay for, but finding the money to do it on my own wasn't easy either.

A few years earlier, while I was still in college, I had spent all of my savings to buy a brand-new Yamaha FZR600 motorcycle. I'd replaced the stock pipe with a carbon-fiber Yoshimura exhaust system that made me feel like I was flying a jet whenever I opened her up. This bike was my baby, but during my time in Japan, I'd had to keep her in storage. At this point, I knew I had to make smart decisions, so I resolved to sell my bike to pay for my private license. It broke my heart, but it was just one in a long line of sacrifices I had to make to achieve my dreams. I was sure it would be worth it.

In late September 2001, I signed up for a private pilot's license course in Georgetown, Texas, thirty minutes from Austin, and began within days of the government reopening flight schools nationwide. My civilian flight training was a complete whirlwind—I studied day and night and spent as much time in an aircraft as I could. I ended up obtaining my license in two and a half weeks, which broke a school record. About three days into my training, it was already time for me to go solo cross-country. "Cross-country" meant that you landed at a different airport from the one where you had just taken off, and for rookie pilots, it was a big deal.

I was ready. I planned out my solo flight from Georgetown to Waco to College Station (Texas A&M University) and back to Georgetown. At this stage, having been training for only three days, I knew very little about flying. Essentially, I knew that you had to navigate by calculating wind direction, and the resultant heading was what you needed to hold for a certain amount of time in order to get to the location you're aiming for. That's it. I knew almost nothing about using my other instruments for navigation. I wasn't flying blind, not really, but when I look back, I'm both amazed and alarmed at how little I knew at the time.

I ran through my preflight checks and took off from the small airfield in Georgetown, Texas. I was more thrilled than nervous—I was finally going up in the air on my own! I had been dreaming of this moment for years.

My leg from Georgetown to Waco was uneventful. I checked in with Houston flight following, like I was supposed to, and the controller replied in an annoyed tone that he saw me. I know Houston airspace is crazy, so I felt a little bad for troubling him. But during my leg from Waco to College Station, the weather started getting worse. The ceiling was getting lower and lower, which pushed my flight path lower and lower, since I wasn't rated to fly into clouds yet. I thought I'd be okay, though, because I was meticulously correcting for the wind and staying on track. Then I was almost grounded by the National Guard.

Halfway to College Station, I caught a glimpse of something out of the corner of my eye. As I turned to see what was happening, two Black Hawk helicopters suddenly appeared, flanking me on my left and right. Houston hailed me on the radio to inform me that I was heading right for Texas A&M University during a football game. Since 9/11, there had been a restriction on aircraft flying too close to large gatherings of people. I was to divert my course immediately.

I complied, my heart pounding wildly, and I soon realized that I would be so far off course that I would have to recalculate the route, which I couldn't do while flying so close to the ground, under the weather, by myself, with only eight hours in my flight-time logbook. I turned around, waved at the helicopters, and quickly went over my options. I probably should have just flown back to Waco, but since I was more than halfway to College Station, I wasn't sure I'd have enough gas. There was also the worsening weather to consider.

In my head, I hurriedly calculated an educated guess as to an alternate route that wouldn't put me too close to the stadium. Then I reluctantly called the air traffic controllers in Houston on the radio.

"Yes, Cessna seven six November . . . Go ahead," he said, sighing.

"Houston, Cessna seven six November . . . um . . . Be advised . . . Well . . . I'm a student pilot on my first solo cross-country, and that divert I just made has knocked me off course. The weather is getting worse, and I'm not 100 percent sure I can find College Station now."

Luckily, Senior Master Sergeant McCabe had taught me that asking for help was a strength. Admitting I was out of my depth was a good thing, I had learned.

In the tense silence that followed, you could sense the shift in the Houston Air Traffic Control facility as the previously annoyed controller suddenly made me his top priority.

"Uh, copy that, Cessna seven six November. Squawk 'one two seven six' and ident for me." This was his way of trying to find me on his radar. I flipped the switch on my transponder that made me light up on the controller's screen for a moment, and he confirmed he could see where I was.

"Okay, Cessna, come left another five degrees to heading one three zero. Check in with me again in one five mike. I'll get you a weather update."

Relieved that someone was going to be able to talk me to my destination, I let out a breath I didn't realize I had been holding. I'd just calm down, follow his heading, then check in with him again in fifteen minutes and hope for the best. But then things got even worse.

"CESSNA SEVEN SIX NOVEMBER, HOUSTON . . . ARE YOU THERE?" The uncharacteristic near panic in the controller's voice scared me out of my momentary calm.

"Yes! Houston, Cessna seven six November . . . I read you."

"Cessna, you dropped off of my radar." He sighed. "Your transponder must be malfunctioning. Recycle and ident." But despite multiple attempts at troubleshooting, we couldn't get my transponder to function consistently. We both slowly realized the situation. I was off his radar and entirely on my own.

"What do you see around you?" he asked.

"Well, I'm in the middle of nowhere . . . Cows?"

He chuckled. "Anything else?"

"I'm just about low enough to read street signs, but no. I don't see anything else." I took a deep breath. I could do this.

I knew I could. "I'll be okay, though," I reassured him. "I know I can find it. I'm sure I'll at least see the town soon."

Unable to do anything else, the controller replied, "Well, you were on a good course last I checked. Hang in there. I'll call ahead and tell them to be on the lookout for you. Good luck."

I'll tell you a secret—you never, ever want to hear the words "good luck" from an air traffic controller. Luck should have nothing to do with it.

I was totally on my own. I regripped the yoke and furrowed my brow in determination. Fear was never a part of the equation for me as I faced moments like this. For some reason, in the moment, I always immediately go into laser focus. It's not until after the incident that I allow myself the adrenaline rush of fear. That day, in that moment and in that aircraft, I was experiencing my first laser-focused life-or-death situation.

Comparing every landmark I could see to the map next to me, I breathed steadily as the cloud ceiling got lower and lower. I looked for any action I could take to help me land before I ran out of fuel, but unfortunately, after only two days of instruction, I didn't have the knowledge to use the various pieces of navigational equipment at my disposal. After about twenty minutes, though, through the mist of the lowering clouds, I finally saw the airport beacon. It was the most beautiful thing I'd ever seen.

I let out a gasp of relief and called out my intentions over the radio to land. Once I had touched down at the airport, only then did I let myself finally feel the weight of what had just happened. I parked in my spot and called for gas. Then I climbed out of the aircraft, knelt on the cement, and kissed the ground, laughing. This would make for a great story when I got to talk to my instructor again.

I was suddenly starving, so I decided to grab a bite to eat. It was the best-tasting club sandwich I had ever had in my life. Then I called my school and relayed the tale to my instructor.

"Rent a car and get back here," he instructed. He'd come get the plane tomorrow, he reassured me. But something in me stirred. I wanted to finish what I'd started.

"No. I can totally fly home. I need to fly it home, or I might not be able to climb into another one again," I responded. I could hear him hesitate.

"Are you sure?" he asked me with incredulity in his voice.

I knew that I needed to shake it off and get back in the air. There was no question in my mind that I needed to get back in that airplane. That was where I belonged.

"Yeah, if it's okay with you. They're reporting that it's already breaking up out here."

"Okay, if that's what you want to do . . . I'm sure you've got this." His confidence in me bolstered my mood. I hung up with him and completed a walk-around of my aircraft. Then I climbed back in, started my engines, and taxied out to the runway. It was such a liberating feeling. The moment my wheels left the ground again, I knew that I had found my true calling in life. I wasn't even scared—I was just elated. Years later, when I look back to this moment, all I can think is that if I had known then what I know now about all the things that could have gone wrong, I would have been petrified. At the time I was just thrilled to climb back into the clouds.

The cloud cover was still heavy, though it didn't appear to be getting any worse. But after my experience getting stuck under the clouds and having to fly so close to the ground, I got worried that the weather was going to creep down again. The moment I saw a hole in the clouds, I went for it, executing a sharp climb and darting through the small hole to see what was on top.

Above the layer that was pushing down on me, the skies were a bright, clear blue. When I broke through and looked down, the cloud layer was like a white, fluffy down blanket spread out below me. It was stunning, and my breath caught in my throat.

What I didn't realize at the time, due to my complete inexperience, was that this move was unbelievably dangerous, not to mention illegal. It was incredibly stupid to fly above the clouds. I had gotten the weather reports from the desk in College Station, but I had no idea what it actually looked like in Georgetown. If my home field was covered in clouds, I would be stuck, especially since my transponder was unreliable. I didn't have the training yet to know how to descend through the cloud layer, and I probably would have ended up crashing. But that day I got very lucky—there happened to be a big hole in the clouds around my home airport. I landed uneventfully and cheerfully relayed the story to my instructor.

When I got to the part about climbing on top of the weather, he said, "No you didn't."

"Yes I did! And it was beautiful," I told him, grinning ear to ear.

"You don't understand what I'm saying. NO. You didn't do something so stupid and illegal. Not if you want to receive your private license," he said sternly.

I instantly wiped the grin off my face.

"Oh. Right. I mean, that would have been cool," I said with a coy smile.

He ruffled my hair, and my heart ached at the reminder of my dad. Maybe it was him who'd opened up the cloud layer over Georgetown. I like to think so.

———— ◆ ————

After I got my license, it was time to get back on a plane and head overseas for my second year in Japan. This time my husband, Jack, would join me. He had spent our year apart finishing up school, and I was both proud and jealous of him for getting selected for pilot training straight out of ROTC. Since he was my husband, he would be assigned to my unit in Japan for about a year while he waited for his pilot training class to start in Oklahoma. They called this "casual status," and this meant he'd be rubbing elbows with the pilots in my unit and treated almost like one of them. I was thrilled to start our lives together after a year apart, finally in the same country, both of us following our dreams.

But very quickly it became apparent that I had made a huge mistake. When we had first gotten together back in college, almost everyone I knew tried to talk me out of marrying him, including his own family. I had started dating him shortly after my dad died, and that emotional state, combined with the fact that he was the first guy I had ever slept with, had clouded my judgment considerably. I was young and thought I was in love, though, and I felt like it was just us against the world. No one believed in us, but I did—*we* did. It was romantic, in a way. Now, looking back, it was just naive stupidity.

Once he arrived in Japan and we started our married life together, my optimism dwindled to nothing. Everyone back home had been right about him, and everyone here in Japan thought less of me for having married him. There were more than a few fighter pilots in Japan hoping to rescue me from him, but that wasn't my style. I decided to resign myself to the fact that maybe life was just supposed to suck. I had made a bad decision, but it was mine to live with.

One night, about eight months after he had arrived in Japan, I was in bed reading. For some reason, we got into an argument about Air Force regulations. Jack was asserting that not all regulations were good ones, and he insisted that there were some you could simply turn a blind eye to.

"Wow. I hope you're never a commander with an attitude like that," I retorted, looking back down at my book.

Then, like a bull about to charge, Jack leaned over me, clenching his fists, staring at me, as if daring me to speak again. Panic gripped me. He had lost his temper countless times before, but this time seemed different. Slowly, and without making eye contact, I slipped out of bed. My intention was to pack a bag, not for the first time, and go stay with a girl-friend of mine who lived nearby.

But as I slowly stepped by him, I suddenly found myself on the floor. It took me a minute to figure out how I had gotten there. Shocked, I looked up, realizing that he had kicked me in the back and sent me flying into a dresser. I'd bounced off the dresser and landed on my butt. I'll never forget that moment, looking up at him from the floor in utter shock.

There was no fear in me—honestly, I was prepared to kick his ass—but it was such an enormous emotional betrayal. Had he come to think so little of me that this was how he felt I deserved to be treated?

In that instant, he saw it in my eyes—the second I had decided to divorce him. He dropped to his knees crying, apologizing over and over. I got up and cradled his head to my chest. We both knew it was over. His temper was something he had struggled with his whole life. He had once told me that he was afraid to get married because of it and that he didn't deserve me. I only wish I had listened to him.

———— ❖ ————

Over the next few days we had countless agonizing conversations, but my mind was already made up. I would not repeat my mother's mistakes and wait for the situation to get even worse. Jack cried as he begged me not to leave him, which surprised me. I always felt as if he treated me like he hated me.

It quickly became obvious as he pleaded his case that he was even more concerned that I not tell anyone that he had kicked me. He was ashamed of himself, and he was probably worried that it would hurt his career. We only had a few months left in Japan, and honestly, I didn't know how to go about divorcing him when we were living out of the country. I didn't want to go through the base's legal services, so I agreed to let him continue living with me until we got back to the US. But from that night onward, we were never really husband and wife again.

After the incident, to be honest, I felt a huge sense of relief. I was devastated, of course, but in some ways, the road ahead was clear for me. I could focus all of my energy on accomplishing my goal. There wasn't time for grieving. It was time to get back to work.

At this point, I had put my pilot application package together, and I couldn't wait to interview with my chain of command. I knew I had a very good chance of being named to the number-one slot off of the base for selection to pilot training, and my hopes were high. Sure enough, my squadron commander easily gave me his number-one rating.

The next step up would be meeting with my Group Commander to convince him to do the same, and I was excited to get the chance to talk to him about my aspirations. After all, he was an F-16 pilot himself. My interview with him went extremely well, but at the end he told me he couldn't in good conscience give me his number-one rating. My throat closed. I tried not to show any emotion, but inside I was panicking. All of my hard work was circling the drain again. How had I screwed up? What had I done wrong?

"But why, sir? Who's your number-one applicant if not me? Is anyone else in your group even applying to pilot training?" I asked, forcing myself to stay strong and not let my voice falter.

"No. You've been an amazing asset to this group. It's just that your husband is here on casual status, right?"

This could *not* be happening. Wordlessly, I nodded. As far as anyone at work knew, we were still together. Jack had stayed on to finish the year, even though we both knew our marriage was over. This was the consequence of my trying to do Jack a solid by not letting anyone know what he'd done.

"Well, how's that going to work with both of you as pilots? Who's going to watch your kids? What if you both get deployed? If he's going to be successful in the Air Force, he'll need a strong support system at home. Don't you want to be a good wife to him?"

My heart sank. It was absolutely none of his business that we were going to get divorced anyway. None of this was any of his business. It clearly was not his place to be making that kind of decision for my family, or anyone's family.

Stunned, I couldn't even respond. I left the meeting and made it back to my office, trying to keep it together. Senior Master Sergeant McCabe saw me return and asked me how it had gone. I told him the whole story in a monotone reenactment, looking down at my desk in disbelief. He grew quiet and his cheeks started to get red. Oh boy. I had seen that before. I knew I was about to get an ass-chewing and guessed I should have stood up for myself more. I gritted my teeth, preparing to get berated. But instead of laying into me, he got up from his chair and gestured for me to follow him.

"Come with me," he snapped.

I followed him right into our Squadron Commander's office. He knocked once on the door, and our commander invited us in. "What's up, Matt?"

"Tell him what you told me," he said to me. I relayed the story to my Squadron Commander, and he silently exchanged a glance with Senior Master Sergeant McCabe. He told me to go back to my office and wait for his call. I don't know what he did, but I'm sure the words "inspector general complaint" probably came out of his mouth at some point during his conversation with our Group Commander, who was his boss. After thirty minutes sitting alone in my office trying to reconcile myself to the fact that I'd be spending another year trying to be number one, there was a knock at my door. I cleared my throat and tried to compose myself, but I couldn't hide my complete shock to see my Group Commander, a full-bird colonel (as opposed to the "light colonel" we called the lieutenant colonels), with his flying gear on and his helmet in his hand, standing at my office door.

"Lieutenant Jennings, I don't know what I was thinking. Of course you have my number-one rating. I shouldn't take your husband's career into consideration when making a decision like that. You're my best officer, so you get the number-one recommendation. You can move forward for your interview with the Wing King. I hope you get it. You deserve it."

I don't know if he said those things out of fear of reprisal for his behavior, or if he really believed it, but I was so relieved. I wasn't dead in the water. I had the green light to go on to the last hurdle, an interview with my Wing Commander, the top-ranking guy on the base. If it went well, I had hopes of receiving the number-one spot from the entire wing, if not the whole Pacific Air Forces.

My interview with the Wing Commander, again, went really well. However, I'd soon be walking out of his office after taking yet another punch to the gut. He cleared his throat and looked me in the eye.

"MJ, you're clearly the number-one choice, but you're only twenty-five. You have so many years of eligibility left. There's another candidate on the base who's about to age out, and this is her last chance. I'm giving her my number-one recommendation." My heart dropped. I knew there were other men and women on the base who wanted to go to pilot training, and I could understand his reasoning. I didn't agree with it, but at least this wasn't personal.

"But will she be as competitive of a candidate as I will?"

He didn't respond. It was clear his mind was made up already.

I knew that the number-one rating was nowhere near enough to get selected. It was true that there was no way of getting selected if you were number two, but even if you were the number one, it wouldn't be easy. There would be a number one from every base, nearly seventy across the world, competing for only a handful of slots. It was almost impossible to achieve even as the number-one choice.

None of this mattered, though. It was clear I wasn't going to change his mind, and I had to live with his decision. Gathering myself up for the long walk back to my office, I resigned myself to another year of working my ass off to try to be my next base's number one all over again.

My next assignment was Whiteman Air Force Base in Knob Noster, Missouri. I'd be in command of troops who would be working on the B-2 Stealth Bomber, and by God, I was going to be the best company-grade officer that base had ever seen.

——— • ———

In April 2002, I arrived in Missouri to join the advanced team of maintainers who were responsible for the B-2 Stealth Bombers. I knew it was going to be a tough few years, as the program was under constant scrutiny.

Before leaving Japan, I had given Jack the option of divorcing quickly and getting it over with or waiting until he was finished with pilot training. I still considered him a friend, and I didn't want to be the reason he did poorly in training. This was a small concession on my part, since we'd be living apart either way, and I wanted to focus on work. I was certainly in no hurry to date anyone else, and I figured it was the least I could do; he was still devastated by our breakup, whereas I was already feeling stronger. He asked that we wait until after pilot training, so I settled into my assignment at Whiteman, ready for a solitary lifestyle while he finished up his pilot training in Oklahoma.

Helo pickup.

Once I started at Whiteman, I worked my ass off and quickly gained the esteem of the aircraft maintenance leadership. Eventually I was assigned the absolute best job that someone in my position could hope for. I would be in command of the Fabrication Flight, which at any other base meant keeping up and patching the skin of the aircraft. A high amount of work goes into maintaining the stealthy skin of the B-2, so at Whiteman, about 85 percent of all B-2 maintenance falls under the Fabrication Flight. It was a very prestigious job, which also included briefing distinguished visitors, such as congressmen, generals, and admirals, as well as being called into key conversations around the deployability of the aircraft into a given military situation. My flight comprised more than two hundred military troops and thirty-seven civilians.

When the B-2 went into its first-ever combat deployment, Operation IRAQI FREEDOM, this mighty aircraft was responsible for the majority of the shock and awe of the first few weeks. It couldn't have been a better time to be in charge of the Stealth maintenance at Whiteman—what an incredibly opportune moment to have this job on my résumé. I was definitely looking forward to this year's application for pilot training.

A few months later, when the application process began all over again, I started checking off the boxes. For example, every year you had to obtain an exhaustive flight physical. This physical included a gynecological exam, but since flight surgeons weren't gynecologists, each year I'd obtained the necessary exam and tests from my military ob-gyn doctor. Then I would submit the results to the examining flight doc. The previous four times I had taken a flight physical, twice in ROTC and twice in Japan, this had been completely acceptable. But that year at Whiteman, for some reason, the flight surgeon decided that this was no longer acceptable.

Dr. Adams, one of the many flight docs on the base, was in charge of my flight physical that year. He conducted a thorough exam, much more thorough than I was used to, as his attempts to ensure I didn't have any "tumors" led to him groping my breasts far more attentively than seemed absolutely necessary.

"Okay, put your feet in the stirrups," he commanded.

"What? No, you don't understand," I protested. "I just had an exam. I gave the paperwork to the nurse at the front for your review."

"No, YOU don't understand," he said angrily. "You're not in charge here. You don't get to decide how this goes. I won't sign off on a physical that I don't conduct myself, and if you want to be a pilot, you'll PUT your FEET in those STIRRUPS. NOW."

I could feel the color drain out of my cheeks, and I felt like I was about to throw up. He was a general flight doc, not a gynecologist. I tried to explain to him that my husband was the only man who had ever seen me naked, that I had only ever had female gynecologists, and that I didn't think this was necessary.

"Please, sir . . . Can't you just use the exam I had last week?"

He looked at me like I had just slapped him. Then his God complex kicked in.

"No, but what I can do is fail you for psychological reasons," he barked. "You don't have the mental toughness you need to be a pilot if you can't submit to a simple exam. If you don't get your feet in those stirrups in five seconds, you can kiss being a pilot goodbye."

I lay back and put my feet in the stirrups and began to cry, involuntarily squeezing my knees together, dreading the exam. It was bad enough having a female doctor examine me, but a male? No man other than my husband had ever touched me there. I bit my lip and tried to tough it out. *He's a doctor. He knows what he's doing. He does this sort of thing all the time. It'll be over soon.*

Dr. Adams snapped his glove on.

"I guess you're not going to like this," he said, chuckling.

What followed was in no way a gynecological exam. I lay there crying so hard I couldn't even breathe as he aggressively and painfully conducted his "exam," as if he was trying to embarrass me, to hurt me, to put me in my place, to assert his control.

To this day I can't explain the emotions of that horrible moment, as many times as I've gone over it in my head. He was a doctor and a superior, and he had complete control over my future. That was the day I learned that mental restraints can be as tight as physical ones.

I couldn't believe this was happening to me, but I didn't feel like I could stop him. I was in shock. I just stared at the ceiling, tears streaming down my face, praying the torture would be over soon. Obviously if I had known he would do this, I never would have allowed it, but now I felt powerless to stop it. It was without a doubt the worst few minutes of my life. When he was done, he pulled off his glove and walked out of the examination room with barely a backward glance.

"Get dressed. We're done here," he snapped over his shoulder.

I pulled on my clothes, still choking back sobs, petrified I had failed some sort of psychological test. I couldn't hide my tears as I walked out of the medical facility. While I was worried that I might have failed my flight physical, I was also fully aware that someone had just used his position of authority to sexually assault me.

Would he still fail me? Had I cried too much? Was there

anything I could do? Should I tell someone? I was in shock. Just then an airman ran up behind me, calling my name. I was in such a terror-stricken state that I flinched and put my arm up protectively. She froze and took a step back, her eyes wide.

"Captain Jennings, the Med Group Commander wants to see you in his office," she said quietly. "Can you follow me?"

In a daze, I followed her to the full-bird colonel's office, not really caring about what he could possibly have to say to me, terrified I would bump into Dr. Adams again. Was the Med Group Commander going to tell me I had failed my physical? That I had to submit to a psych eval? I was shaking and still crying as I tried to salute him. He stood and walked over to me, returning my salute.

"Are you okay?" he asked kindly, his brow furrowed, concern written all over his face. "Here, have a seat."

"I'm fine," I said, wondering why he was concerned, how I came to be sitting here when this terrible thing had just happened to me. I was nowhere near ready to talk about it, certainly not to him.

"Well, you don't seem fine." He shook his head. "I just talked to Dr. Adams. He came straight from his appointment with you to tell me what he'd done. Do you want to press charges?"

My head started spinning. The doctor had already admitted what he did? I had just left the examination room five minutes earlier, and things were happening so quickly. Before I even had a chance to answer him, my own Group Commander walked through the door.

My commander sat down with us, and the three of us discussed my options. I was so embarrassed to be discussing this with two old men I barely knew. I could press charges if I wanted to, but if I didn't, they'd be sure to "handle it." I began crying harder. Then I listened in disgust as I uttered lines that seemed to come straight out of a made-for-TV movie.

"If I pressed charges, would I have to see him?" I sobbed. "Would I have to tell a roomful of people what happened?" I was shaking, horrified with myself for being so weak and not standing up for myself more, but still I said no, that I didn't want to press charges. If they promised not to let him ever do it again and that they would punish him "their way," I'd leave it in their hands. I trusted them.

"I think that would be best. And don't worry . . . He's not failing your physical," my Group Commander reassured me.

I admit, I was relieved to hear this. Instead of being utterly furious and ready to fight this monster, to end his career, part of me was just relieved that I'd passed my physical and I could still move forward with my dream to become a pilot. I simply wanted to forget absolutely everything that had just happened.

I asked if I could go and walked out without further discussion. Over the next few days, I called in sick to work and spent the time alone in my house, crying nonstop, unable to sleep or eat, replaying the horror over and over in my mind. I knew I needed to talk to someone about it, but I couldn't bear the thought of anyone knowing I had let this terrible thing happen to me. I couldn't stand to see the look of pity on their face. So I turned to my best friend in the world.

I spent a lot of time curled up with Jäger those awful few days, his long white fur soft under my fingers. He nuzzled me with his sweet piggy snout while my tears drenched his coat and I told him all of the things I was scared to admit to anyone else. He listened quietly, and his soft eyes seemed to say, *I don't know what you're saying, but I promise everything's going to be alright . . . And if I ever see that guy, I'm going to bite his balls off.* There was a reason he was the only guy I trusted.

After a few more days of this self-imposed isolation, I knew I needed to leave my room, to get back out in the world, but I could just barely summon the strength.

When I did finally return to work, my Squadron Commander, Major Busch, looked at me with knowing eyes. Clearly he had been briefed. He asked if I was okay, and I responded simply with an apology for missing work.

"Don't worry about it. You can take some more time off if you need to." The last thing I wanted was to keep crying at home. I needed to start moving past it, and the best thing I could do was to get back to being the best maintenance officer I could be, knowing I'd need to fight even harder for the number-one slot this time around, but also secretly wondering if I even wanted to be a pilot anymore.

A few months later I was selected as the Operations Group Company Grade Officer of the Year. It was decision time. This honor would definitely help my chances at getting the number-one slot off of the base, but my commitment to the

Air Force was up in a few weeks. I could either apply again for pilot training, or I could get out of the Air Force entirely.

I really struggled with the decision. After my assault, my trust in the Air Force had taken a nosedive, but I knew I had a chance at the number-one slot and that I could be back on track for my goals in no time. I also knew that if I left the Air Force, it wouldn't mean giving up my dream, as I could always apply with the Air National Guard. I really didn't know what to do. My Squadron Commander, Major Busch, tried hard to talk me into staying, and it felt good to be so valued by someone I respected, someone who knew me.

At the awards banquet where I was set to receive my honor, all of the group-level awardees were dressed in formal wear, gathered with our respective commanders. I sat at the banquet table chatting with Major Busch when something out of the corner of my eye caught my attention. Dr. Adams was there, dressed to the nines, with his boss.

"Holy sh*t," Major Busch sputtered. I had thought it, but Major Busch had said it. Dr. Adams had been selected as the Medical Group's Company Grade Officer of the Year. I would be competing with him for the wing-level award.

My jaw dropped, and I looked over at Major Busch, who was wearing the same expression on his face. He could see in that instant that I had made my decision.

I didn't even say anything.

"I know," Major Busch said. "I'll help you with the paperwork."

I don't know who won the award that night, but it wasn't

either of us. Disgusted with the way the whole thing had been handled, with Dr. Adams's chain of command protecting him this way and even rewarding him, no doubt for his so-called honesty, I tried not to blame the entire Air Force.

It was hard not to. It was the general culture of the Air Force that had given Dr. Adams the idea that he could treat me like that. Clearly he was right. He could and he did, and he was never punished for it.

I left the Air Force a few weeks later. Dr. Adams, as far as I know, stayed on.

THREE

THE LAST FEW WEEKS of my Air Force career were spent
sending in my applications for pilot training with various
Air National Guard units around the country. My soon-to-be
ex-husband, Jack, had graduated from pilot training, so I
also began the process of filing for divorce. When he received
the paperwork in the mail, he called me from his base in
Little Rock, Arkansas, and actually had the gall to sound
surprised.

"But I haven't hit you in over a year!" he said to me. Un-
believable. I mean, was he serious? We hadn't lived together
for a year and a half. I had seen him now and then for things
like the ceremony where he got his wings, but we hadn't spent
any actual time together. I guess he had managed to convince
himself that I wouldn't go through with it. But I knew staying
in that marriage would have been a slap in the face to my
mother and all the sacrifices she had made to get me away
from my biological father. She had found happiness after her

first marriage. Maybe I could someday, too. Despite his incredulity, I assured him that I definitely still wanted a divorce.

In March 2004, I was ecstatic to get a call from the New York Air National Guard offering me a pilot slot to fly Combat Search and Rescue, or CSAR (pronounced "see sar"), HH-60G Pave Hawk helicopters. Simultaneously, I was also offered a spot to fly A-10s by another guard unit. I couldn't believe it. I had always wanted to fly the A-10. An agile, low-altitude attack aircraft, the A-10 represented my personality better than any other airframe. The aircraft itself was designed and built around its enormous 30mm cannon, offset from the center of the nose due to the propensity for the weapon to actually turn the aircraft when fired. Finally. After all of the obstacles and roadblocks, it was happening. I was going to be a pilot.

It was an easy choice. I called Lieutenant Colonel Mike Noyes in New York—he had become somewhat of a mentor to me through the application process—and let him know that, while I was grateful for the opportunity, I was going to take the A-10 slot.

"Why?" Lieutenant Colonel Noyes asked me. I was a little taken aback with the question. I figured anyone would take an A-10 over a helicopter.

"Well," I answered, "I've always wanted to fly the A-10."

"Yeah, but why? What about the A-10 do you like?"

What was there not to like about the A-10? There was no way he was going to convince me that the A-10 wasn't the best airframe in the inventory.

"I love the flying profile. They're just off the deck, directly supporting ground troops, incredibly maneuverable, and the sound of the gun just gives me chills. It's as close to being 'in the sh*t' as you can get as a pilot."

"True," he said, "but you can get all of the same stuff you're talking about with us. And here's the real bottom line. We're a search-and-rescue platform. As an A-10 driver, you'll be spending all of your time training and maybe someday deploying to use your skills real world. With us, you'll be doing real-world missions all the time. You could be doing a local flight and get called out for a rescue any day of the week. We do water rescues . . . We put out wildfires . . . We support local law enforcement. Oh, and we also go to war and get in the sh*t with the ground troops. You'll be saving lives. Can you do that in an A-10?"

I got chills. It was like he had flipped on a light switch in my soul. He was absolutely right. All of the excitement and impact I was looking for was right here in front of me. I couldn't believe it, but I was going to turn down the A-10 slot and sign up with New York.

My life was starting to look up. I was newly single, driving a new motorcycle (a Yamaha R6 with, of course, a Yoshimura pipe), getting off of active duty, and about to live my dream. I was so happy about embarking on my new career.

Barely able to contain my excitement, I placed a phone call to Keenan Zerkel, my old frenemy from maintenance training, to tell him about my pilot slot. On the second ring, he picked up, sounding just as excited as I was.

"MJ! I'm so glad you called! I have news!" he said.

"Me first!" He was going to flip!

"Okay, go."

"I GOT A PILOT SLOT!" I yelled as I bounced up and down.

"ME TOO!" he replied.

"No sh*t? Really? That's amazing! I'm joining the Guard, though."

"Cool. Me too!" Zerk replied.

"Wow, that's weird. I'm gonna be flying rescue helicopters . . . ," I began, wondering what the odds were that we'd both get this once-in-a-lifetime chance at the same time.

"Oh crap. Me too!" he said. *Okay, now he's just messing with me, right?*

"Who with?" he asked.

"New York. You?"

"Aww, that sucks. I was about to get excited. I'm gonna be flying for Alaska."

There were three Air National Guard units who flew the HH-60G Pave Hawk, which was the only airframe being used for Combat Search and Rescue by the Air Force: New York, Alaska, and California. In hindsight, of course, it all sort of made sense. We were both hard-chargers who knew we'd eventually get to pilot training. Both of us had applied every year while we were on active duty. It made sense that we'd both get off active duty at the end of our commitment and start looking at the Guard. What was amazing was that we had both picked the same airframe. It was a natural choice for him since he was from Alaska, but for me it was just a happy coincidence that I was going to be flying in the same rescue community as Zerk. We finished catching up, promised to try to see each other soon, and signed off. The next part of my life was about to begin.

———— • ————

I moved back home in March 2004, while I was waiting to begin pilot training in October, and spent a few months in Austin. I swam in Barton Springs by day, then rode my sport bike to my bartending gig on Sixth Street by night, generally just having an absolute blast. But as happy as I was, the time quickly came for me to pay my dues in New York.

In May of that year I got a call that the New York unit was able to find me a job up there so I could get settled while I waited for pilot training to start. I was perfectly happy waiting in Austin, but I was afraid that if I told them that, they would never send me to training. While I had officially been offered and accepted a slot, they still had a lot of discretion when it came to which candidates they sent to one of the various pilot training bases and when. Technically, they could change their mind at any time. I knew they planned to send me to Columbus Air Force Base, Mississippi, soon to begin my eighteen-month training, but I felt like first I had to show them that New York was my new home and that I'd do anything to be a part of their family.

So I quit my job, packed up my car, hooked up my motorcycle trailer, and got on the road. The worst part was that I had to leave my sweet puppy, Jäger, with my mom. If all went well, I would be in New York for a couple of months before pilot training started. During pilot training, I'd be staying in a dorm and moving every six months or so to a different location. I knew that wasn't an ideal situation for a dog, so my mom was going to dog-sit until I was finished with training. I'd come visit him as much as I could throughout training, but I knew I would miss him terribly.

The drive from Austin to New York City takes about three days. There was a moment a few hours into the trip when I came upon an on-ramp to Highway I-40. The sign said turn right for New York or turn left for Los Angeles. New York or Los Angeles.

I had everything I owned in my car, and it felt like the first time in my life that I had no commitments whatsoever. I could literally just turn left and have a completely different life. Of course, my dreams lay ahead of me in New York, but it was really liberating to finally feel like I had a choice. After more than four years of being told what to do in the Air Force and four equally draining years in an oppressive marriage, I finally felt like my life was my own.

I couldn't stop smiling as I gripped the wheel and turned right. I would be in control of my life from here on out. I'd had enough of doing things just because I was expected to. I would never again let someone treat me like dirt. I would never again let someone convince me he could do whatever he wanted to my body against my will. I was truly free.

———— • ————

As much fun as I'd been having in Austin, it turned out that my time in New York was even more amazing. I was making a fourth of what I had been making in Austin and paying three times as much for living expenses, but I didn't care. I was in New York. My dreams of actually living in the city itself were dashed when I realized just how far out on Long Island the unit was, so I began house-hunting for something in my budget a little closer to where my job would eventually be. There wasn't much to choose from, but I knew I'd find the right place if I just kept looking.

About halfway down my list of a dozen or so apartments and guesthouses, I hit the jackpot. Someone had renovated an old fourteen-by-fourteen-foot railroad maintenance repair shack. Inside was a single room with a tiny bathroom just big enough for a toilet and a standing shower. A sink and a half-size college-dorm refrigerator for a kitchen completed the floor plan—and it could be mine for a cool twelve hundred dollars a month. No closet, no TV connection, one window, and no neighbors—my dream home. When the owner showed me the shed next door and informed me I could park my motorcycle there if I could get it inside, my decision was made. Sold.

I built a ramp so I could park my bike in the shed, set up my futon as both a couch and a bed, and used an upside-down laundry basket as a coffee table. I had all I needed and had never been happier.

I got a night job bartending at a local restaurant called the New Moon in East Quogue, and the staff there started calling me "Austin." It was a BBQ place, so I suppose I was lending

Pave Hawk.

some Texas credibility to it among the customers. The owners were great, and the customers were not what I expected. As opposed to the trust-fund babies I thought I'd have to deal with in the Hamptons, our clientele was more like the people who worked hard keeping the rich people on Long Island happy.

I spent most of my free time when I was off work either rock climbing in the Catskills or climbing on top of my motorcycle shed, sitting on the roof, and enjoying a plastic cup of whiskey with a cigar, listening to my blaring music from the open window of my own private railroad shack, missing my dog.

My training wouldn't start for another few weeks, so I didn't mingle with the aircrew much—I wasn't really one of them yet. But soon after I arrived in New York, I did get to bartend for the retirement of one of my heroes, Lieutenant Colonel Dave Ruvola, who would be retiring before I had the chance to fly with him. He was a gorilla of a man who had shown he was a true hero during what became known as the Perfect Storm—the real-life disaster that the film was based on.

After attempting a boat rescue and being thwarted by the worsening weather, Dave and his Co-Pilot, Graham Buschor, were caught in the worst possible situation. Out of fuel and trying to head back to their base, the crew tried to refuel off of a C-130 airplane in the middle of one of the worst storms on record.

Unable to "plug" their refueling probe into the small round cage attached behind the C-130, Dave had to make one of the toughest decisions a pilot ever has to make—either keep trying and likely crash when the engines flamed out, or use what was left of his gas to execute a controlled ditch into the ocean. But with seventy-foot swells, under night-vision goggles, this was a lot harder than it sounded.

Trying to save his crew while risking being dragged to the bottom of the ocean, Dave ordered the men on his aircraft to bail out as he tried to hold a steady hover. In a previous career, Ruvola had been a Pararescue Jumper or PJ. One of the many skills of a PJ is to be a rescue swimmer who trains to save people from stormy water. He knew he'd have a better chance of surviving the plummeting aircraft than the others. After hours stranded in the freezing water, he managed to find two of his crew in the pitch-black storm, tether them to himself, and swim to a nearby Coast Guard ship. A fourth member, Graham Buschor, also managed to make his way to the ship. Sadly, the fifth, PJ Rick Smith, was never found. It's thought that he may have dropped from the aircraft at the trough of a wave and fallen seven stories to his death in the water, but no one will ever know for sure.

Ruvola is the type of hero you read about or see on TV, not the kind of person you expect to see dancing to "YMCA" during his retirement while you serve mojitos. Meeting Dave and interacting with such an amazing man affected me profoundly. I'd call upon the memory of his example later in my own career when I was tested and faced with daunting odds myself.

About a month before I left for training, I was walking into a local Laundromat with a laundry basket in my arms when my phone rang. It was my mom, and she was crying so hard I could barely understand what she was saying.

"Mom? Are you okay? Is Jäger okay?"

"I'm so sorry, baby," she wailed unintelligibly. "He died."

I dropped the basket in the parking lot and just sat next to it and cried. I never should have left him, even though I knew he'd have been miserable in New York. I couldn't believe he was gone, that I hadn't been there to comfort and hold him at the end. Apparently, his scarred and enlarged heart had finally given out, and he'd died in his sleep.

I was utterly heartbroken. My best friend was gone. It was as if I were experiencing all of the grief of losing my dad all over again, but Jäger, at least, had known exactly how much I loved him. I had learned that lesson from losing my dad.

In October of 2004, heartsick from losing my Jäger, I packed up my shack, put some of my belongings in storage, trailered my R6, and got back on the road to the first stop in the training pipeline, Columbus Air Force Base. The months I'd spent in New York before attending pilot training had given me a sense that I didn't deserve to walk the same halls as pilots like Dave Ruvola . . . yet. Now I was off to Columbus, Mississippi, to begin my training—determined to earn my place among my heroes.

———— * ————

When I arrived at Columbus, I could feel my heart lift as I drove through the front gates. I was finally here, and just in the nick of time. I was twenty-eight years old, within months of the maximum age limit. I took a deep breath as I began looking for signs pointing to my dorm. I pulled my burnt-orange Honda Element, peppered with Longhorn stickers, into a parking spot outside my assigned room. The dorms on the base were really more like small 1970s apartments, with more isolation and privacy than a regular dorm. The doors opened up to the outside, motel style, rather than opening to an interior hallway.

My arms overflowing with trash bags filled with my belongings, I nudged open the door to my room with my foot and peered inside. Only slightly bigger than my shack in New York, the tiny room was painted a drab tan, and the carpet was disgusting. But I was so thrilled to finally be here that I would have been happy to sleep in a sleeping bag in the parking lot. I dropped the bags onto the bed and plopped down next to them, looking around the room that would be my home for the next six months. I heard a few of the guys who were my neighbors walk by laughing, and I stifled the urge to jump up and meet my fellow pilot candidates. I wasn't there to socialize, and my experiences with military men were not all that positive thus far. That would change when, in the coming years, I would fly into combat with some of the finest men and women I'd ever meet, but at this point I was happy to sit quietly and steer clear.

Training would begin with weeks of academics in a classroom before we would get anywhere near an airplane, but even in the classroom, our fortitude would be tested.

My first true test came during our introduction to survival training in the first week on the base. Our instructor had a swagger born of the confidence that comes with having trained hundreds of people to survive in the wilderness. Survival is all about your attitude, he explained. "Captain Jennings, can you humor me for a minute?"

I swallowed nervously as I looked up to meet his eyes. I hated being singled out, but I walked to the front of the classroom, looking around at my forty classmates, trying to put on a brave face. It was then that I realized there was only one other woman in the room.

I stood in front of the class as the instructor continued talking.

"So you've ejected from your aircraft and you're waiting to be rescued. No one comes, and it's your third day out there on your own. Captain Jennings, can you reach into this cup and pull out what you find?" He held up a paper cup above my eye line.

I could feel something slimy and immediately realized it was a fat worm about a half inch thick. No problem. I could do this. Just as I painted my tough-guy face on, the six-inch worm wrapped itself around my finger. To my utter disappointment, I shrieked and dropped the worm on the floor. The class laughed as the instructor explained that I'd never survive, due to my prudish American food aversions.

Not five seconds after I had dropped it, I bent over, picked up the worm, rolled it between my palms, and tossed it back like a shot of whiskey.

"Mmmm. What else you got?" The class roared in laughter and cheered me on.

I noticed, as I returned to my seat, one of my classmates looking a little green. I patted his back and said with a gentle smile, "Don't worry. I'm sure we don't all have to do that." He glanced at me, grateful for the support.

The instructor struggled to continue making his point, disappointed that I wasn't the easy mark he'd thought I would be. To his credit, he turned it into a learning moment anyway.

"Which brings me to my next point," he continued. "Never judge a book by its cover. Sometimes the biggest asset on your team isn't the one who looks like Superman. People will surprise you with the strength they can summon when tested."

Over the next few months of training, we'd experience some of the most fun and the most challenging moments of our lives. For example, because the T-37 Tweet we'd be flying for this first phase of training was an ejection-seat aircraft, we needed to learn how to land safely from a bailout. They literally tied us to the back of a pickup truck with about a hundred-foot-long rope, strapped us into an open parachute, and dragged us until we flew up into the air like a kite. Then they disconnected us from the truck, and we had to execute a safe landing—what we call a PLF or parachute landing fall. We had already practiced on the ground from ever-increasing heights, by jumping off of a jungle-gym-type of structure, but it was truly thrilling to try it from one hundred feet under an actual parachute.

Most days after class, I'd drive out to the approach end of the runway and sit on the hood of my car, listening to the radio calls made by the students ahead of us in the rotation who were already up in the air. I had bought a radio that would let me pick up the transmissions so I could get used to the verbiage and timing of the calls. Sitting out there at sunset, doing what we called "chair-flying," I still couldn't believe I was finally in pilot training. As I sat there, I would chair-fly the pattern they were flying, imagining myself going through the motions: checking airspeed, lowering gear, lowering flaps, and running through checklist items that would one day be second nature.

We worked hard and played hard during training. My memory of spending Halloween in New Orleans that year is pretty fuzzy, but I know we had a fantastic time. As much fun as we had, though, we knew we'd be miserable if we pushed it up too hard on a work night, and as one of the older students, I rarely made that mistake. Occasionally someone would show up for class in their blues uniform stinking of whiskey with bloodshot eyes, but for the most part, we were pretty smart. We knew how fragile our hold on this dream was, and we knew we were already incredibly lucky to be there. No one wanted to risk ending that for something stupid, so we all took good care of each other when we were blowing off steam.

After weeks of academics and flight simulators, it was finally time to head out to the flightline. I remember this part of training as the most eye-opening and exhilarating time of my life. My first time flying a jet was mind-blowing. Taking off was like sitting on a controlled explosion and rocketing up to our block of airspace. Doing it solo was certainly a thrill, and executing the acrobatic maneuvers approaching 250 miles per hour was as close to heaven as I will likely ever get. It's difficult to pinpoint a favorite activity while flying the mighty Tweet, because I loved every minute of it, but the spin training might have been the ultimate highlight.

During this phase of training, we would purposely put the aircraft into a spin. Think of it like practicing skidding on ice in a car, in order to learn how to control something that feels completely out of control. Of course, in the air, it's at an exponentially higher level of magnitude. This maneuver would never be done solo—it was always with an instructor.

Spin training accomplishes a few things all at once. First,

obviously, it teaches us how to recover from a spin. Second, it shows us how to recognize the warning signs of a stall and familiarizes us with the feeling in the aircraft so that we can avoid it. The higher the angle of attack (the angle the wing makes to the wind), the less efficient the aerodynamics of lift is. At a critical point, all lift will break away from the wing; pilots call this a "stall." Over the years, there have been far too many deaths attributed to students stalling the aircraft in the slow turns we take around the pattern before landing, so spin training has taken on an elevated importance. Finally, it teaches us aircraft handling techniques and gives us a hands-on understanding of the performance of the aircraft.

When we do spin training, we start off by going full speed up to a high altitude. I watched carefully until the altimeter needle began to struggle as we neared twenty-five thousand feet. I pulled up the nose as our airspeed began to bleed away; the stall-warning horn started screaming and didn't stop. I was pointed sixty degrees nose up, sky filling the entire windscreen, slowing from two hundred miles per hour to about fifty and about to lose all the lift from my wings. On purpose.

I held the nose up with the stick and tried to stay level as the plane began to shudder and climb higher and higher, fighting the stall for as long as I could. Finally, physics won and the left wing dropped, beginning a spin and a rapid descent toward the ground. Ten thousand feet per minute sped by the smooth glass of the canopy. From the ground, the jet must have seemed like a figure skater spinning and dropping head-first from a cloud.

As the blue and green lines of the horizon twirled around at a disorienting speed, I focused on my instrument panel, breathing evenly.

I eased back on the throttles and put the rudder and ailerons in neutral position at the same time. Then I yanked the stick full aft and pushed the rudder to the floor in the opposite direction of the spin. After another turn, I pushed the stick full forward, marveling at the amazing performance of this beautiful aircraft.

As I recovered from the steep dive and high airspeed, the aircraft stabilized. My instructor and I were back to comfortably cruising along at a mere 180 knots and fifteen thousand feet. Primal exhilaration filled my chest. I felt like screaming in victory.

I looked over at my instructor with a grin plastered across my face.

His fists unclenched.

"Wow," he boomed into my headset, "that was the best spin recovery I've seen . . ."

My smile stretched.

". . . from a chick."

Damn.

Pilot training wasn't all adrenaline-filled acrobatic stunts. There were painful, tedious parts as well. The students ran the morning briefing, where we would take turns speaking to the class about the weather, the schedule, and other key information. This was boring but also highly stressful, as the instructors critiqued us while the other students sat at attention, observing. The majority of the students in the class were fresh out of ROTC or the Academy, and as such were very green second lieutenants. I had five years in already, so I wore captain bars on my shoulders.

As the highest-ranking student, I was appointed the class leader. I tried hard to think of a way to cut the tension during the morning briefings without disrupting the learning. A few of us decided that we should begin a word-of-the-day competition. The challenge would be to attempt to use the word in the morning briefing without arousing any suspicion among the instructors.

This worked for a couple of weeks, but it soon became too easy. In our prebrief meeting, I knew it would be my turn to speak that day, so I felt like upping the ante a little bit, just to keep everyone on their toes. I looked around the room at the tired, stressed-out kids in the class, my mind racing. When someone asked what the word of the day should be, I quickly responded, "How about *flaccid*?" My classmates chuckled.

"Do you dare me?" I added. Realizing I was serious, one of the older guys who was in training to be a KC-135 pilot for the Air National Guard quickly shook his head. "No. No, we do not dare you." The rest of them were a little more adventurous and were more than happy to dare me.

As a Guard pilot, I had a huge advantage over the rest of the class. The active-duty pilot candidates were still competing for a class ranking, as I had so many times before. At the end of training, the school would give the number-one student first choice of the available aircraft. If there was only one F-16, for example, the number-one person could take that and there would be no other F-16 pilots from our class.

However, things were different in the Guard. Because my unit flew HH-60 helicopters, I already knew what I was going to end up flying, so I wouldn't have to compete for the airframe I wanted. The warrior in me wanted to fight to graduate at the top of my class anyway, but I was willing to risk getting in a little bit of trouble with my instructors if it cut the tension for a few minutes for everyone. The instructors filed in to listen to my briefing. My classmates sat up at attention, wondering if I'd have the guts to go for it.

"Good morning. Aircrew brief for Friday, March twenty-ninth, is as follows," I began. "Weather is good with unlimited ceiling, clear visibility, and flaccid winds at about five knots from two seven zero . . ." Despite their best efforts, a few of my classmates cracked smiles, and the instructors began looking at each other. I finished the brief, and everyone went about his or her daily schedules. I couldn't believe I had gotten away with it.

"Jennings. My office. Now," my Flight Commander's voice boomed over the top of everyone's heads. Sh*t.

I got my ass handed to me, but it was worth it. I could tell that my Flight Commander knew he had to ream me, but the corners of his mouth kept turning up in a slight smile. He ended up "punishing" me by having me brief for the rest of the week, but after my time in the Air Force, briefing congress-men and generals on the status of the B-2, it wasn't much of a punishment for me—I had no problem with public speaking. Anyway, it was a small price to pay to show my class that they could still have fun when they're under stress. In fact, I found we all performed much better if we could find a way to cut the tension.

The KC-135 pilot candidate who had told me not to mess around during briefings was a good example of this. After a particularly grueling check ride (a flight that is basically a test from start to finish), he returned to our class and threw his checklist across the room. Two of us quickly jumped up and escorted him into an auditorium before an instructor saw him losing his sh*t. Once inside, he kicked a chair so hard I thought it was going to be ripped out of the frame that bolted it to the floor. It was apparent the flight hadn't gone very well.

"I can't do this!" he yelled, his cheeks bright red. "I'm not going to get my wings."

"You're going to be okay," my other classmate told him. "I'm sure MJ can talk to the commander and get you another chance," he continued, trying to comfort him.

Honestly, I couldn't bring myself to agree. I had seen this student continue to maintain the bare-minimum standards while letting every ounce of stress get to him. Despite my compassion for him, I knew he would one day be asked to refuel his aircraft over a combat zone. How would he deal with the stress of getting a surface-to-air missile shot at him while refueling an F-16 over Iraq? Who would be there to boost his confidence and assure him that it would be all right then?

Luckily, I didn't have to decide whether or not to fight for him. Soon after that flight, he withdrew himself from training. I had learned that the warrior spirit and the nerves of steel you needed to fly planes were not characteristics you could predict by gender or any other demographic. Some people just don't have what it takes to do what we were being asked to do, to do what some of us had dreamed about our whole lives.

Of course, there were plenty of times that I found myself wondering if I would make it. There are always moments when you question whether it's worth it or whether you are good enough. Some of us could find our way back from those dark moments, and some of us couldn't. I had no idea at the time just how much I would be tested, but each challenge I put behind me made my confidence grow incrementally. Meanwhile, I was having the time of my life.

———— • ————

Nearing the end of the T-37 phase, I was really in my groove. Of course, I made plenty of mistakes. For example, I "hooked" my first check ride, which meant I failed the flight. It was a stupid mistake, but I learned from it and recovered well in the next attempt. Now that I no longer needed to sit and listen to radio calls to prepare for when I'd be making them myself, I spent most nights studying.

Each night I'd take a break to go for a run around the outside of the flightline so that I could still be motivated by

MJ solo in her T-37.

the beauty of the red and green lights on the aircrafts taking off and landing during their night phase. But the recurring knee injury, the one that had sidelined me in ROTC training years earlier during college, still plagued me. The pain grew steadily throughout my nightly runs, but I stubbornly and stupidly pushed through it.

Finally, two weeks from finishing up the T-37 phase of my training, it got to the point that I couldn't even climb into the aircraft. I went for an assessment and received the bad news that the pain wasn't due to the injury. It was actually a recurring condition; my kneecap was being held down too tightly by my tendons, so my cartilage kept tearing, leading to chronic pain in both of my knees. The fact that I had broken it in college on the obstacle course made it worse, but there was nothing to be done. I was told I would need to undergo surgery to loosen the kneecap in order to walk without pain.

I was furious at myself for ignoring the pain and continuing to run at night. I met with my Flight Commander to discuss my options. I was so close to the end that we decided it would be best to go ahead and finish training. I would just have to climb on the plane through the instructor's side so I could use my good leg on the foothold we used to pull ourselves into the cockpit. The alternative—to suffer through a minimum six-week hiatus and possibly come back with stale hands, having lost the sharpness from my studying—was a nonstarter. I took the first option and finished the phase, limping out to the line each day.

I had the surgery at Columbus, and after just three weeks of recovery, I was sent straight to the next phase in my training. I left Columbus Air Force Base for Fort Rucker, Alabama (affectionately known to the pilots as Mother Rucker), to continue my training. This phase of training was similar to the T-37s in that it started out slowly, all academics in classrooms. Then finally, when we moved onto the flightline portion, it was absolutely exhilarating.

Apparently I was supposed to do my physical therapy while simultaneously trying to learn a new aircraft, but instead, stubborn as ever, I slacked off on the rehab so I could focus on the training. This felt like the right decision at the time, but it would come back to bite me soon enough.

At Fort Rucker I'd learn how to fly the mighty UH-1 Huey. I couldn't wait to get my hands on one. The classic muscle car of helicopters, the Hueys we'd be flying had been in Vietnam, and the patched bullet holes in the fuselage were a sobering reminder of why we were here in the first place. It was during my Huey training that it began to sink in that I wasn't just here to fulfill my dreams; I was here to serve my country. I'd be flying alongside the Dave Ruvolas of the world and trying to save people's lives, and despite my enthusiasm, I was taking that very seriously. I was here to soak up every bit of knowledge and skill I could from my instructors.

During the academic phase at Fort Rucker, I had an incident with one of the civilian instructors that was a humbling reminder of how much more I had to learn. One day the instructor said something I disagreed with. Obviously, as a student, I should have listened to the instructor and let it go, but instead I was disrespectful and pushed back, a little too hard as it turned out. I had given in to a feeling that most of us feel at one point or another in training—that one of our instructors didn't know what the hell he was talking about. After the altercation, I quickly realized my error, and I wrote the instructor a letter. It was an unequivocal apology, because I was truly embarrassed that I had been disrespectful to him. On my way into another class, I handed it to him with lowered eyes.

Later that day, our class instructor, Captain Randy Voas, showed up outside one of my classes. Captain Voas was amazing. He had flown spec-ops helicopters in some of our country's lesser-publicized "incidents," and he was the perfect mix between being a badass and simultaneously really caring about his students. I couldn't help but think that his wife and two little girls had humanized this tough guy. He was truly one of the best instructors I knew throughout my entire training experience.

When Captain Voas showed up outside my class, he opened the door to the classroom and simply pointed to me. I jumped up and joined him in the hall, nervous at being pulled out so conspicuously. He was holding my letter in his hand. I was sure I had messed up by putting the incident in writing, basically confessing to disrespecting an instructor. Oh God.

"SEE THIS?" he yelled at me. Gulp.

"Yes, sir," I meekly answered.

"THIS just SAVED your ASS. We were talking about what to do with you after you mouthed off to Mr. Jeffries, and the consensus was to kick your ass out of training. It was the end of the dream, Jennings, but the humility and authenticity in this letter has swayed the group. You get one more shot, but DON'T F**K IT UP!" He turned on his heel and stalked off.

As he walked away, I felt myself start to shake. I couldn't believe how stupid I had been, how close I had come to getting kicked out after all I had been through to get there. Stunned, I went back into class a different student from the one who had come out. I would listen to and respect my instructors much more from here on out.

———— ⊛ ————

When we started the flightline training on the Hueys at Fort Rucker, I was in heaven. The low-level night-vision-goggle navigation training was the most dangerous thing I had done in my life, and I loved every second of it. After a twenty-minute flight, we had to hit our landing zone within thirty seconds under low illumination with simulated enemy forces popping up to engage us. It was beyond stressful and absolutely amazing. Completely at home in the environment and eager to soak up every ounce of knowledge, I was having more fun in this phase of training than I ever thought possible.

It was during this phase I learned what autorotation is. Sometimes as a student, you'll be flying along, minding your own business, when your instructor will reach over and just cut off your engine. To the untrained eye it looks like we're just flying straight to a crash site, and that's sort of what it feels like at first, too. Technically, the engine just goes to idle, so you could turn it back on if absolutely necessary, but you're supposed to act as if you've lost your engine. This is called autorotation. The rotors immediately slow, as the aircraft feels like it just deployed a drag chute. It's as if you're going 120 miles per hour on the highway and you blow all four tires at once. The student dumps the collective (the horizontal stick on the left that controls the power), which puts less demand on the rotors but makes the aircraft fall like a rock. This also makes the rotors spin faster as they store the kinetic energy. This is a good thing, as you'll need that stored energy to keep you from crashing at the bottom.

As you turn the aircraft sharply (you don't want to stay in a turn during this maneuver, as you'll drop faster) to land facing into the wind, you have to somehow gain control of the aircraft in order to put it where you want. It feels like you're riding an angry stampeding bull and you somehow have to get him to calm down and go through a specific gate before you fall off.

As you approach the ground, first you have to go nose up in order to bleed off your airspeed. Then, before you lose all of your energy and fall onto your tail, you level off and ease the aircraft to the ground. It slides on its skids across the runway, sending sparks into the air as you slowly come to a stop. This is the part when you look up at your instructor with a grin, excited that you're both still alive. Then he looks at you and shakes his head as he writes down all of the things you did wrong. It's one of the best and worst moments in training.

After each flight, there would be a grueling debrief. This is the part of the flight where the crew talks through every moment, from the preflight brief to the postflight walk-around aircraft inspection. There were many things we were graded on. Some were specific, things like the ability to hold your hover within ten feet or your airspeed plus or minus five knots. Others were general impressions by the instructor, like "situational awareness" or "judgment." I did pretty well in pilot training, but I certainly made my fair share of mistakes. I was no stranger to constructive criticism, but I didn't "hook" many flights (that means to get a "U" or an "unsatisfactory," which is basically a fail).

My main instructor was Mr. Edmunds, and I am a much better pilot because of him. A Vietnam-era Huey pilot, Mr. Edmunds has forgotten more about helicopters than I will ever know. He was tough but fair, and I wanted nothing more than to get his stamp of approval. I knew from the beginning how very lucky I was to have been assigned to him, and I hope I made him proud later in my flying career.

There was one day of training when I most definitely did not make him proud. It was a pretty rough flight where nothing seemed to go my way. It was one of my off days, but you can't afford to have those as a pilot. There'd be no sympathy for having a "bad day" out in the real world.

After the flight, we hovered back to our parking spot and landed. As the rotors spun down, I took off my headset and looked to my left over the center console to see his reaction. His slight frame and bushy white mustache gave no indication of his opinion of the flight, but his silence was deafening. I watched as his hand flipped switches on the upper console on the roof of the cockpit, when he suddenly made his hand into a "U" and sort of let it drop and bounce as if it were on a bungee cord until it was right in front of me. This was his way of saying I had hooked the flight, and if I wasn't so devastated, it would have been pretty funny. I took a deep breath and unbuckled my seat belt. *This debrief will be fun*, I thought.

Later, walking out of the debrief with my head down, I bumped right into someone and bounced off his barrel-chested flight suit. I looked up, pissed off.

"Heh-heh . . . Holy sh*t. What up, MJ?" It was Keenan f**king Zerkel. I threw my arms around him, and he picked me up and swung me around.

"Zerk! Oh my God, am I glad to see you. I've had such a sh*t day and could really use a drink."

He had just arrived from his T-37 phase in Oklahoma, and I was excited that our timing was so perfect. Our Huey phases would overlap by a couple of months. We made plans to hang out and blow off some steam, and since I was a few weeks ahead of him, I told him I'd give him all the "gouge" I could, which meant passing on notes and tips for him and his class-mates. It was really great to see a friendly face amid all of the stress and competition. I couldn't believe he was there. It'd be like doing maintenance training all over again, only this time we were friends.

When Zerk and I met up later that week, I told him as much as I could.

"If I have only one piece of advice for you," I told him over a beer, "try to get Mr. Edmunds assigned as your civilian in-structor. I've learned so much from him."

Not all instructors were as useful as Mr. Edmunds, though, and an instructor named Captain Jones was one of the least useful. I would fly a kick-ass flight with him, knowing that even Mr. Edmunds would approve, and yet every single time I flew with him, he'd hook me. And every time, I would rack my brain to try to figure out what I was doing wrong so that I could become a better pilot, but he'd never be specific with me about how I could improve.

After each flight, I'd read my training record. And every time, he would mark me down as failing one of the subjective things like "judgment." After the third flight I hooked with him, I was fed up. I'd only hooked four flights in my whole time there: the one time with Mr. Edmunds, and the other three with Captain Jones for "judgment" or "situational awareness." Finally, I went to the Director of Operations (DO) to ask for his advice. I had flown with him as well, and he knew me to be a good pilot.

The DO assured me he'd get to the bottom of it and asked Captain Jones to join us. It didn't take long before he admitted the real reason. Captain Jones "didn't like me," he said. His religion didn't believe in divorce, and he thought I should be taking care of my husband instead of being here. He also didn't think women should be flying. I stood there in shock, not just at what he was saying, but at the fact that he felt safe saying so in front of the DO. Surely his career would be over. Or at least his time as an instructor, right?

Wrong. My grades stood. He was never admonished, not that I saw. He continued to be an instructor, flying with my male classmates. The only thing that was done was to ensure that I was never scheduled to fly with him again. After the incident with Mr. Jeffries that almost got me kicked out, though, I wasn't about to rock the boat.

Looking back, part of me regrets that I didn't make more of a fuss, but I knew the time wasn't right. Later in my career, when I had more credibility, I would have a lot more leeway to create change. Back then I simply had to put my head down and be grateful that Captain Jones had not succeeded at failing me out of training for my gender.

Nearing the end of training, Captain Voas slapped me on

the shoulder and said, "Christ, Jennings, you really ended up kicking ass. I'm proud of you." I tried not to let him see my eyes well up. This was the next best thing to my dad being there to say it, the moment I had been hoping and waiting for. He didn't know it, but that moment meant even more to me than actually getting my wings. Years later I learned that Captain Voas was killed in Afghanistan flying the V-22 Osprey, and I immediately thought of his wife and kids. The world lost a great man that day.

Graham Buschor, the Co-Pilot on the Perfect Storm mission, agreed to come to Mother Rucker and officiate our graduation in January 2006. It was an incredible honor. Receiving the top academic award in front of him was just icing on the cake. I think I would have gotten the top stick as well if it hadn't been for the three hooks Captain Jones had given me, but it didn't matter. Getting those wings pinned on my chest was all I wanted, and it meant I had won. I blew him a kiss as I walked out of the hangar. I was on top of the world.

———— • ————

That night I threw a big party at my apartment for my class. I couldn't believe I was finally a pilot in the Air Force. We'd all be going to survival training soon, so we wanted to celebrate before heading off to hell. Survival Evasion Resistance Escape—known as SERE and pronounced like "sear," as in "searing pain"—scared most of my classmates to death. We had all heard the stories of starving in the woods, getting the crap beat out of you by mock enemy interrogators, and the

MJ receives the top academic award.

like, but I was really looking forward to it. I couldn't wait to get there and learn the skills I'd need to be an even better pilot.

I got dressed for the party in a fantastic mood. I threw on a tight pair of jeans and silky sleeveless top with my leather motorcycle boots before starting to make some Jell-O shots. As it turned out, my illustrious past as a bartender really came in handy during pilot training. My classmates showed up along with students from the classes behind us, and we started to celebrate. When the door slammed open with a bang, I didn't need to look up to know who it was. Zerk never knocked. He ambled into my place and high-fived me. Now the party could really begin.

A few hours later, I needed a break from all the revelry. I walked out to my balcony, which was on the third floor, enjoying the glow of the Christmas lights strung out along the roof. I stood there in the chill, gazing out at the stars. January was a little too cold for a sleeveless shirt, even in Alabama. I wasn't out there long before the door opened and Zerk ambled outside, the music trailing behind him. Closing the door after him, he joined me at the railing. He didn't have to ask me why I was out there. Zerk knew me well enough to know that I loved a good party, but I was still a complete introvert. I always needed to find a quiet place to recharge my battery.

He and I chatted for a while about how excited I was to be going to SERE training and then on to Albuquerque for the last few months of HH-60G Pave Hawk training, the third and final phase of pilot training. Having finished the Rucker phase, I had already received my wings, but I wouldn't be qualified as a rescue pilot until I got through Kirtland Air Force Base in Albuquerque, New Mexico. Zerk had a few months left, but he'd be in Albuquerque soon enough.

I'm sure it was equal parts alcohol, the relief at finally having received my wings, and my loneliness after having married the wrong man, but when Zerk put his arm around my shoulders to try to warm me up in the chill night, it felt very different from the dozens of times we had hugged before. I sensed his breathing change as well, and we turned toward each other at the same time. Looking at him, his big, strong arms holding me tight, I felt safe. That's the last thing I should have felt, as I knew Zerk was like the Big Bad Wolf, but I couldn't help it. I liked being in his arms.

He looked down at me. I looked up into his dark eyes.

"Proud of you, kid," he said quietly.

He knew better than anyone the things I'd had to overcome

MJ is sworn in by Graham Buschor.

to get here. I tilted my chin up as he leaned down to kiss me, and the sparks flew. I'd figured he would be a great kisser, and I was right. The kiss quickly turned more passionate, and he scooped me up and sat me on the railing. He knew full well I was an adrenaline junkie who loved heights, so this move just about sent me over the edge, literally and figuratively. I wrapped my legs around him and made sure there was no space between us.

But right about then, we both seemed to have the same thought. We were way too close to have something meaning-less, but not nearly close enough for something serious. There was clearly an undeniable attraction, but that was all it could ever be. We were married to our pilot wings, and neither of us would ever sacrifice our careers for the other. We chuckled as we untangled ourselves, and I hopped down to the porch.

"Wow," he said.

"Yeah, wow," I agreed. "So, um, can I get you a drink?"

"Definitely," he said, glad that I had said something first, I think. We rejoined the party, trading smiling glances for the rest of the night, and never spoke of that kiss again.

FOUR

IN JANUARY OF 2006, I packed my bags for Survival Evasion Resistance Escape training. SERE evoked in me an odd combination of fear and eagerness, as it is one of the most thorough, useful, and sought-after schools in the Department of Defense. We often have people from other branches fighting for SERE slots, and every Air Force pilot has to finish it in order to be operational and have any hope of ever deploying to a combat zone. It's easily one of the most difficult and daunting courses offered by the military, albeit not as long as the more well-known, grueling schools like the Army Rangers and Navy Seal training.

I knew SERE training would be an important step in my effort to mold myself into the combat warrior I hoped I could be. It would be an amazing opportunity, but it would also be the most difficult thing I had ever experienced. I was anxious and exhilarated and excited and terrified, all at once.

One of the things that scared me was the fear of the

unknown. Most people are very closemouthed about what happens at SERE, and this is for good reason. To prepare our combat warriors for the possibility of becoming isolated behind enemy lines, it's essential that those heading to SERE have no idea what they're getting themselves into. If and when you become a prisoner of war, one of the most terrifying aspects is not knowing what will happen to you. The curriculum at SERE is intended to mimic this experience as closely as possible, so this sense of disorientation is important.[1]

When I arrived at Fairchild Air Force Base in Spokane, Washington, it was with a fair amount of trepidation. As the second-highest-ranking person in my class of about seventy, I already knew I would be put in an unenviable position later in training. When the group was divided in half, I'd be in charge of one of the two flights.

We began, as usual, with academics, where I soaked up as much knowledge as I could. This phase wasn't about competition or "passing," and it was difficult to be kicked out of this portion of the pilot pipeline. That's not to say there was no attrition. A lot of people can't take this type of challenging environment, living off of the land and being chased by bad guys, and they would self-select out. They can't see the value

---

[1] I would advise anyone reading this who may be going to SERE at some point in their career not to read the next couple of pages. I also advise you to resist the temptation to research and find out what it will be like. I won't include anything in this book that's not available on the internet (posted by people who have shared experiences on blogs and such), and my account has been cleared by the DoD for release, but if you go to the training with an idea of what to expect, you're doing yourself a disservice. By the end of the course, you will not be as well prepared for the future as the person standing next to you.

of this rare chance to hone and develop your skills as a war fighter; nor can they see the light at the end of the tunnel. This is fine, though; none of us wants someone on our wing who can't handle this type of stress.

After the classroom portion of the training was behind us, it was time to head out into the Pacific Northwest woods. For the first couple of days, it would still be somewhat of an academic environment, only now we'd be freezing our butts off outside instead of being stuck in a classroom.

It was a frigid February morning when we headed into the woods, armed with only what we could carry on our backs. There was a foot of snow on the ground, but you could still smell the earthy scent of the forest. I watched as my breath turned to mist in front of me. Once we arrived at the foot of the first mountain, we were broken up into elements of seven or eight people. My group had a broad range of ages, genders, and skill sets, so I knew we'd be a strong team. One of my crew was a technical sergeant (TSgt) who was a thirty-eight-year-old chain-smoker. I earmarked him as someone I'd need to keep an eye on, but secretly, I was glad that I wouldn't be the one holding us up on the difficult treks ahead.

As we unloaded from the vehicles, the instructors handed out the items we would be using our first day. My classmates and I formed a line from the bus and handed equipment down the row. Whatever you ended up with, you carried to the first camp. I thought I had lucked out when someone handed me a warm, snuggly little bunny rabbit. He must be our mascot! My instructor warned me not to name him, but of course as soon as he said that, I immediately picked a name for him. I couldn't help it; it just popped in there. It was like Dan Aykroyd and the Stay Puft Marshmallow Man. Our mascot's name would be Bugs.

Bugs nuzzled into my shoulder as we trekked up the hill to our first camp. When we arrived, I was loath to put him down, but when the instructor put a second bunny down as well, I followed suit. When he began describing how we would need to kill and dress the animals we would catch, I locked eyes with Bugs. Oh my God. This was freaking SERE. What had I been thinking? Of course he wasn't our mascot. We were going to eat him.

After a long description of the most humane way to kill an animal (which I barely heard, I was so busy having a silent panic attack), the instructor lifted the second bunny by his back feet and hit him in the back of his neck hard with a big stick. It sure didn't seem like the most humane way, though. The bunny didn't die but instead let out a scream I will never forget. It was the most devastating noise I had ever heard. The instructor managed to kill him with his second hit, but we were all rattled.

Bugs, who was visibly shaking, hopped over to me and nuzzled his face into my ankle. I looked up at the instructor, my eyes welling up with tears I couldn't hide.

"That's why we don't name them," he said with a chuckle. "Don't pick him up."

Now and then, throughout the rest of training, I thought about Bugs and how sweet he was. And I hate to admit it—after a few days of not eating, that rabbit tasted delicious. But the episode gave me a real appreciation for the hard decisions I'd have to make as a leader to ensure the survival of my crew.

———— • ————

During the first few days of SERE, our instructors showed us how to assemble a shelter, build a fire, and catch and dress food, among other lifesaving skills. They certainly didn't give us much time to practice, though. Within a few days of arriving, each team was handed a map and a compass and told that we had just crashed in enemy territory. We would have to navigate our way to a mock pickup point where we could expect rescue. For our first time out, they were nice enough not to surround us with instructors pretending to be enemy forces, not just yet anyway. First we would have a little time to get the hang of land navigation and survival. But we all knew that the evasion phase, where our instructors would essentially be stalking us, trying to "kill" us, was right around the corner.

We took turns being in charge of navigation. In those first few days in the woods, I learned one of the most vital leadership lessons of my career—namely, that being "in charge" in this type of scenario didn't mean you made all of the decisions. It means you select the *right* person to make certain decisions. The best hunter in the group, for example, should be the one to set the traps.

Some of the troops in my element were terrible at navigation, but they were here for training just like the rest of us. The upside was that while they tried their hand at navigation, we all learned from their mistakes. On one leg in particular, a young lieutenant among us decided it would be faster to go over one of the giant hills in our way rather than around. I mentioned to him that the lines denoting elevation on the map were awfully close together, but he felt like we could handle it. I glanced at the chain-smoking technical sergeant and saw that the despair on his face mirrored mine. I shared his doubt, but it was the lieutenant's turn to be in charge, not ours.

We angled toward the hill as our instructor shook his head in disapproval. The young officer would need to learn this one the hard way, by driving his element into a very difficult position. The special-operations guy in our group was clearly equipped to tackle the hill in front of us, but he seemed well aware that the rest of us would likely need help.

As we started up the hill, my pack seemed to become heavier with every step. Although it had seemed manageable thus far, it weighed in at fifty pounds, and I was starting to realize that I could probably do without half of the equipment it contained. The terrain began to steepen, and it wasn't long before we found ourselves using our hands to get up the hill on all fours. By the time we were about two-thirds of the way up, the incline was already at about seventy degrees, and my fingers ached as they dug into the frozen terrain. I could hear the spec-ops guy helping the technical sergeant carry his pack, but I was determined to do this on my own. My thighs burned, and I could feel my left knee weakening. With each step, the pain in my post-op knee became more and more unbearable.

The hill had gotten so steep, we were no longer hiking; we were rock climbing. I rested my forehead in the dirt inches from my face, sweat coating my forehead despite the frigid temperature, and took a deep breath. Then I kept moving. I refused to stop. *Just take one more step. Everyone has one more step in them. Okay, now just take one more . . .*

"Hey . . . Are you okay? Give me your pack!" I heard ahead of me. It was one of my teammates, but I waved him off and took another step. He grew more insistent as I got closer to the top, as the rest of my element was already up there. I was not going to give in. As it became apparent that I was determined to do this alone, they began cheering me on. My body felt like it was going to fail me at any moment, but sheer will finally pushed me to the top. I rolled over onto my back, propped up by the pack that I now despised. I couldn't feel my left knee, but that was a blessing. The spec-ops guy crouched down next to me.

"Well done. That was one of the most amazing things I've ever seen," he said, nodding his head in appreciation. "You really looked beat about thirty minutes ago. It's like you got up that hill on sheer determination. I don't know how you did it. Kick ass, Captain. That was great."

I smiled but stayed silent, glancing around at the view, my chest pounding with pride and exhaustion. It was beautiful up here, though the sparkly stars that looked like fireworks across the picturesque landscape might also have been a sign that I was about to pass out. My team started to gather their gear together now that we were all up the hill. I needed about a day to recover, but there was no time. We had a rendezvous to make.

As I gathered my things together, my pride quickly started to wane, however, when I realized what I had done.

My stubbornness and determination to prove I could do everything without a hand up had cost us precious time. This would be by far the most valuable lesson I would learn at SERE. Sometimes you have to set your ego aside and do what's best for the group. The guys had no problem helping one another out, and it was ridiculous that I acted as if I had something to prove. I would spend the rest of my career trying not to make that mistake again.

As my group finally neared the rendezvous, we broke up into teams of two. The "evasion" phase had begun. Instructors dressed in black were creeping throughout the woods ready to pounce on us if we made a single mistake and showed our position. My partner and I moved silently through the woods, stopping to listen every now and then, crossing roads tactically and covering our tracks. We looked at our map and spoke only in whispers, deciding on the best route to take around an open field. When we heard voices approaching us from the right, we immediately hit the deck. That was when I felt my knee blow out. Something had clearly destabilized, and I found myself lying there on the ground in excruciating pain. I moved my foot back and forth to test the knee. Sure enough, something was really wrong.

If I had mentally been in training mode, I probably would have raised the time-out signal and sought medical attention.

But I was so engrossed in the scenario that I felt as though I had to stay silent. After about fifteen minutes, I heard a scratching by my feet, then felt a nudge at my boot. I thought we'd been captured, but instead of an enemy soldier, some sort of rodent scurried up my leg, over my pack, over my head, and into the field. I let out a little surprised yip.

The rodent was followed shortly thereafter by the instructor, who had snuck up on us. "Nicely done, Jennings," he said with a laugh. "When I saw that squirrel run up your leg, I thought for sure you'd scream. Now, GET ON YOUR KNEES, AMERICAN SCUM!" I struggled to kneel with my hands on my head, but the pain was too extreme.

The instructor quickly broke character and began to assess my injury. In the cold weather, I was wearing several layers, including bike shorts, so I lowered my pants to get a good look at my knee. The kneecap had moved about two inches over to the outside of my knee. You didn't have to be a doctor to see that it was in completely the wrong place.

"Ooooh, that doesn't look right," the instructor said, grimacing. He called for a medic on his radio, and I was carried to the road we had just crossed and loaded into an ambulance.

The medic's assessment was that the surgery I'd had, the one that was meant to loosen the tendons that held my kneecap so tightly, had caused instability in my kneecap. The combination of the surgeon cutting too much and my lack of real physical therapy meant that my knee just wasn't strong enough to handle the stress I was putting on it out here in the field. I would essentially be kicked out of SERE (despite having already finished the majority of my training) and allowed to come back only after some intense rehab. I was headed home. Again.

The instructors who rode with me in the ambulance explained the process to me and looked at me with sympathetic eyes. They warned me that most people in my situation never complete SERE. I would have to start all over, and apparently it was far more difficult to return when you knew what you'd be in for.

I looked at them defiantly. It didn't matter to me what "most" people did. I wasn't most people. I assured them I'd be back, and they shared a glance. They clearly didn't believe me. I didn't mind; they obviously had no idea who they were dealing with.

Luckily for my career, since I already officially had my wings, I had some leverage. Instead of disqualifying me immediately, the Air Force just focused on getting me better. I was sent back to Mother Rucker in Alabama for four months of intense physical therapy. I'd serve the training squadron in an administrative capacity and fly whenever I could to stay current, but my job was to get better. I received another slot for SERE in June, four months from now. That would be my last chance.

Luckily, I hadn't moved out of my apartment yet. I kept it for another four months while I did my rehab, and I attacked physical therapy with an intensity that bordered on obsession.

At SERE with MJ's evasion partner.

If the therapist asked for ten reps, he got fifteen. If he asked me to do a wall squat (where you sit like you're in a chair with your back to the wall) for a minute, I'd push myself to ninety seconds. Then, after my time in the physical therapy clinic, I would keep exercising at home, averaging at least four hours of rehab a day. I was in full-on *Rocky IV* movie-montage mode, and SERE training was my enormous Russian.

In June I headed back to SERE, more excited than fearful. I knew I would pass this time—my body was finally feeling as tough and as well prepared as my mind. Sure enough, my second go-round at SERE was successful, and I completed my training uneventfully. Well, if you call getting starved, chased, and tortured "uneventful."

That summer, I left Fairchild confident that I could handle anything I might encounter when I was eventually deployed overseas to a war zone. The skills and lessons I had learned in SERE were truly life-changing, and in the coming months, I would credit the course and the instructors there for my ability to maintain my composure during the tight spots I would soon find myself in while flying in combat.

———— • ————

The final phase of my training before being considered a fully operational pilot would be at Kirtland AFB, New Mexico, my second time in Albuquerque. I hadn't returned since I'd been there for the Aircraft Mishap Investigation Course and the 9/11 attacks.

During this last phase, we would be introduced to the beautiful HH-60G Pave Hawk helicopter. Flying the UH-1 Hueys at Mother Rucker was like driving a classic muscle car—all rich history and no modern technological conveniences. Stepping into the Pave Hawk, or the "60" as we called it, was like sliding into the seat of a Ferrari. The multitude of systems, radios, and other gadgets was overwhelming at first glance, but it would all eventually become second nature to us.

Lucky for me, it became apparent early on that I was an excellent multitasker. I could be navigating, running checklists, and flipping switches and still be the only one who caught a faint radio call amid the background noise in our helmets. Many studies have shown that this is an attribute that women tend to possess more than men, and in this male-dominated culture, I'd take any advantage I could get.

The missions we simulated in the Pave Hawks were more

complex than anything we had done before, and the gun patterns were exhilarating. We would toss out a glow stick to mark the simulated position of our survivor, identify a tank or something that would serve as our simulated bad guy, and then roll into incredibly fast-paced, tight patterns where we would always have a gun firing on the enemy position. The idea was that between you and your sister ship, someone always had to be raining hate down on the bad guys who were trying to get to our survivor before we could. The whir of the minigun just outside my door always got my blood pumping. I could barely wait to get back home and start flying actual real-world missions.

In January 2007, I reported back to my unit in New York. At that time, casualties were really starting to mount in Afghanistan, and the Air National Guard had been called up to run medevac in Kandahar, the hottest part of the theater. The New York Guard was heavily populated by tough firefighters and cops who were all ready to serve—and I was finally one of them. Deployment day loomed just two months away; I was thrilled and ready to rumble. Then they told me I'd have to sit this tour out because I was so new. I was devastated.

But then they saw me fly. I suppose I had an advantage over the type of pilot they were used to getting right out of training. I had spent some hard years on active duty, and the challenges I overcame, both personally and professionally, had helped me develop a sense of calm under pressure, a maturity, and a level of composure that most new pilots don't have.

I was just shy of thirty-one years old and had gotten a little banged up along the way, but I was finally where I belonged. My chain of command all agreed: I was ready for combat. They would take me with them despite my lack of experience.

The day I got my deployment orders, I called home, excited to tell my mom. When she picked up the phone, we chatted for a few minutes about the usual stuff, and then I gave her the news. There was a long silence, but instead of pushing for a response, I just waited.

Finally, she told me that she was both proud and scared.

"I wish David were here to share the news," she told me quietly. "He'd have been so proud, MJ."

I nodded, blinking back tears. I had been thinking the same thing, of course, wishing I could just say, "Can you put David on?" Part of me still needed my dad's guidance, to just have him tell me I was going to be okay, not just good but great. I was about to fly into the mouth of the cat, as the Vietnam-era vets like David would have said. I could have used some wise words from a brave, seasoned veteran before heading off into the unknown.

But my dad was always there with me; I knew he was watching, somewhere up there playing fetch with Jäger. I carried them with me in my heart as I boarded the airplane out of Baltimore that would take me into my first real combat zone. I could hear David's voice in my head as I took one last look over my shoulder at American soil.

"Knock 'em dead, sweet pea."

FIVE

WHEN I SHOWED UP to my squadron building in New York in April 2007, I was dressed for the first time in a desert-tan flight suit, feeling strange not wearing my normal olive green. We threw our bags onto the six-by-six square baggage pallet waiting to be cargo netted and forklifted into the C-130. All I had with me for the next several months was a duffel I would carry with me through Kyrgyzstan and into Afghanistan.

I was excited to be deploying with my unit, but I was also a little apprehensive about going into combat with people I barely knew. But by the time I threw my bag on the baggage pallet, I was feeling ready. I had just finished cramming ninety days' worth of local orientation training into about forty-five and rolled right into our deployment spinup training, which took place on and around our base on Long Island.

The spinup training had consisted of a refresh of some skills that we would use in Afghanistan but didn't have much use for in the United States. For example, we practiced what we called "brownout landings." When a landing is made on unimproved surfaces covered with dust and sand, a cloud develops around the aircraft that will blind the crew just as they near the landing pad. It's incredibly dangerous; practicing this critical skill was one way we could prepare ourselves for the conditions we were about to face in Afghanistan. I enjoyed the training and got high marks, but in the rushed runup to deployment, I didn't have a lot of time to bond with my sisters- and brothers-in-arms before heading off to war.

The first part of our journey to Afghanistan would be a bus from the base to a commercial airport. We would then take a short flight from New York to Baltimore, then hop a plane to Frankfurt, Germany, before ending up in Manas, Kyrgyzstan.

When we shifted from the comfort of commercial aircraft to the loud, cold jostling of the cargo bay of a C-130, the mood seemed to change. We were all a bit lost in our own heads, and there wasn't much talking going on. I chitchatted with my new squadron a little bit, but for the most part, everyone on board spent the hours hiding behind headphones, sleeping, watching movies on iPads, or writing letters to loved ones. Seasoned deployment veterans bore glassy eyes and seemed like they were already tired, but I could barely contain my excitement. Trying not to display my rookie status by showing everyone how giddy I was to finally be deploying, I channeled my thoughts into scribbling in my journal.

Our time in Manas was typical of most who have experienced the Kyrgyzstan base. It's a waypoint you have to go through on your trip into the Afghan theater. We were there for a few days, sleeping in a big bay on bunk beds, choking down the food, and trying to relax and pretend we weren't about to go to war. It was disarming to see the über-tough PJs singing karaoke, but in a way it humanized them. These guys were some of the best of the best, the toughest of the tough, but beyond that, I would soon find out that they were, for the most part, incredible guys as well.

PJs are a unique group of people. I like to think of them as a mix between ████████, SEALs, Rangers, Coast Guard Rescue Swimmers, and Combat Medics. They're the Air Force special operators, and they train to be able to kick ass in any environment (sea, desert, mountains), overpower an enemy who is trying to capture an isolated person (such as a pilot shot down over enemy lines), provide medical assistance to that person, and help get their ass out of the hornet's nest. PJs parachute out of planes, fast-rope out of helicopters, and do hundreds of other amazing things on a daily basis.

For our medevac mission in Kandahar, we would be flying with regular flight medics, not PJs. But our PJs were going to be assigned next door to us and would be flying with the squadron pulling CSAR alert. We would see them all the time, but we wouldn't be flying with them. The higher-ups would soon decide that it was too dangerous and decree that we should be flying with a team of PJs instead of flight medics, but for this deployment we would have to settle for seeing them in passing as they came and went from the building next to ours.

The guys next door to us at KAF who would be standing on alert for CSAR would be lucky to have our PJs with them. And while medevac and CSAR may seem similar to the casual observer, the difference between the two missions was monumental.

CSAR is what happens when a good guy is down, hurt, and alone. Usually it's a downed aircraft or an ejected pilot. The person is isolated behind enemy lines with no cover or backup, and the enemy is usually trying to beat us there. We have to go in with guns blazing, find the survivor, protect them, pick them up, and keep them alive on the way to the hospital.

Medevac is when a person is injured and needs to be brought to a hospital, but they are also surrounded by some type of perimeter, like on an actual base or with a convoy providing cover. And while an actual CSAR mission would be more exciting than medevac, I knew we'd be flying more often, so I was happy.

Whether or not we were bringing our PJs was the only X factor. Other than that, the typical crew always has an Aircraft Commander (AC), who is the senior pilot on board, and a Co-Pilot (CP). Both are fully qualified pilots and can interchange duties, but the ultimate decision and responsibility lies with the Aircraft Commander. Normally the AC flies while the CP navigates, but during some of the less exciting times, the AC may let the CP get some flight time. For all three of my deployments, I was a CP. I would upgrade to AC in 2010 but ended up leaving the Air Force before deploying again.

In the back of the aircraft, you would find an Aerial Gunner (AG) and a Flight Engineer (FE). This distinction has since changed, and the career fields have been merged together. In 2007 through 2009, during my deployments, the "backenders," as we called them, would sit in side-facing seats looking out windows over their aircraft-mounted machine guns. The FE was the systems expert who would assist the pilots with checklists, make decisions on how to handle system malfunctions, and other such tasks. The AG was the gun expert; he would mainly man his gun and assist the FE with his or hers if needed.

This is the standard crew that gets rounded out with a medic or a team of two or three PJs, consisting of a PJ team lead and one or two regular PJs. On any given day, you could fly with any mix of crew. However, we tried to keep crews together as much as possible, to develop a rhythm. When you fly with the same people over and over, you run through checklists faster, you anticipate one another, and you form a bond with one another. People who are not used to flying together will still operate well, as we all know our duties, but being "hard crewed" with a group of people is preferable—especially in combat. I was looking forward to figuring out who I'd be crewed with and starting this adventure with some experienced, talented aviators on an aircraft I had completely fallen in love with.

The HH-60G Pave Hawk was truly a thing of beauty. Modified from the UH-60 Black Hawk Army troop carrier, the "60" had upgraded avionics, which gave us the ability to fly into bad weather and nighttime conditions. After all, those are the perfect conditions under which to execute a rescue. We want to capitalize on our technological superiority over most of our enemies by operating in environments that make it difficult to see. In addition to the avionics, search-and-rescue platforms need the ability to fly long hours in order to loiter over a search area or fly out to the middle of the ocean. The Pave Hawk has auxiliary fuel tanks to increase our flight time to about four hours, plus a refueling probe, which gives us the ability to fly until we have to land for fatigue. It was an amazing piece of equipment, and I could hardly wait to start saving lives with it.

———— • ————

As we crossed the border into Kandahar, our C-130 plane went dark to help protect us from any enemy ground troops in the area. The aircraft entered into a rapid descent to get us on the ground as quickly and safely as possible. We knew this kind of landing was standard and most of us expected it, but it also seemed like it completely unnerved everyone. It felt like it was the first time we were vulnerable to enemy fire, and all of us knew it was just the beginning. Welcome to Afghanistan.

As we stepped off the plane, I took a look around me. Dust covered everything and seemed to permeate every pore within seconds of our arrival. It was clear everyone was exhausted from the trip, but processing onto the base went quickly enough, and soon we had gathered our stuff and were checking out the base. We were surrounded by uniforms from other countries and by unfamiliar languages, but this comforted me and made me feel like we were really part of a coalition. We were all dying to investigate our sleeping quarters, ready to pass out, but there was no time for sleep.

Once we had dumped our stuff in the barracks, we met the guys we would be replacing. This unit had been pulling the medevac alert for the region over the last six months or so, and while the Air Force has shorter deployments than the Army, I could still see that these men and women were fatigued. The nonstop flying and constant state of readiness had taken its toll on them, and there was a tiredness in their eyes that foreshadowed what we were getting ourselves into. Needless to say, the unit was all too eager to get us ready to fly, so they were highly motivated to begin our orientation. The sooner we could take over the mission, the sooner they could head home to see their loved ones and knock back a few cold ones.

We were quickly brought up to speed on the local area through academic briefings and familiarization flights. The way "sitting alert" for medevac works is that every twelve hours, at each shift change, the incoming crew puts their gear on the aircraft and builds sort of a nest around their seat, filled with anything they might need to grab, like checklists and equipment. I used to carry the standard equipment of survival gear, signal flare, and first aid kit, but I augmented my vest with things like a rescue knife, which you can use to break glass and cut seat belts, a push knife, a boot knife (I like knives—what can I say?), a handcuff key, extra water and ammo, a flashlight with red and UV interchangeable lenses, and a small metal tube that carried a single cigar.

The cigar was my promise to myself that I would get out of that country alive. I planned to smoke it after my last mission and before the flight home. The last nonstandard item I carried was a folded-up American flag. It made a triangle about eight inches long, and I kept it in a Ziploc bag to keep it relatively free from dust. I planned to carry that flag with me on every single combat mission I ever flew.

During shift change, the Co-Pilot will also power up the aircraft (not rotors turning, but power to the avionics and radios) to align the navigational system, check the radios, and make other such preparations. Then, once the aircraft is prepped, we get off the plane and go into the Tactical Operations Center or "TOC" (pronounced like "clock"). Here we would receive the daily brief, which is when we get all of the up-to-date info on threats and other classified information. We had to do it in this order in case sh*t hit the fan, more politely known as "a mission dropping" during the brief. No matter what happened while we were in the TOC, if we were on shift, we would have to be ready to go in an instant.

A typical medevac mission from Kandahar goes like this: The crew is relaxing, often in the TOC or somewhere nearby, usually having just come down off a recent mission. We sometimes flew as many as five missions in a single shift, so we were always eager for some downtime. We might be reading, playing Xbox, or heading to chow, but we were always alert and ready to scramble. The intel person is sitting at his or her computer, which is set to sound an audio alarm if the words *9-Line* come across the screen. A 9-Line is the list of information we get when a mission "drops" on us. It generally has information like the location, the nature of the patient's injuries, and whether there is any enemy activity in the area. There are occasionally false starts, missions that are aborted before we even get off the ground, where we end up standing down. But for the most part, when the alarm goes off, it means we're about to fly.

Upon hearing the alarm, video games get paused, conversations are hushed, and all heads in the TOC turn toward the intel person, quietly anticipating what comes next. The intel person will look up at the Aircraft Commander or PJ team lead and nod, saying something like "We're a go." Then they reach for a handheld radio to declare, "REDCON ONE! REDCON ONE!"

Ready Condition One means approval to launch, which kicks us all into action. If we had heard "REDCON TWO" instead, that would only give us approval to spin up the aircraft and wait for launch authority. Upon hearing the radio call, the room explodes into motion as everyone heads out to man their position. The aircraft maintainer goes out to address any malfunctions and help the aircraft taxi out, the PJs grab extra gear in response to a unique injury, and the Co-Pilot and backenders hustle out to get the engines started. Meanwhile, the Aircraft Commander is getting as much info as possible from intel about the mission.

By the time the Aircraft Commander and the PJs get out to the aircraft, the rotors should already be turning on the 60, and the rest of the crew is just waiting for them to strap in for the expedited taxi out to the runway. The Aircraft Commander briefs the rest of the crew with as much info as possible about what they're heading into. Then it's wheels up.

A second aircraft, known as your "sister ship," has been going through the exact same motions simultaneously, because in medevac missions we go everywhere "two ship." This ensures that if one of us is shot down, the other can pick up the crew from the crash site, which is called "Self SAR"—in other words, Self—Search and Rescue. The second aircraft is interchangeable with the first, but the Aircraft Commander in the lead aircraft (called the "Flight Lead") is responsible for the entire formation and directs the actions of both birds.

At a designated area "across the fence," the backenders would test-fire our guns with a short spurt to make sure we're good to go. You don't want to find out that your guns are "bent," that is, not working, when you're trying to engage a real-world threat. Then the Co-Pilot navigates the Aircraft Commander around any known or perceived threats, avoiding paralleling roads and other such tactical no-nos. We avoid the "lines of communication," like roads, rivers, and such, to the greatest extent possible because it minimizes our exposure to enemy forces who would shoot at us or report our position to someone.

Most medevac missions tend to be between thirty and sixty minutes, whereas CSAR or even civilian search-and-rescue operations can last several hours. In combat, though, our flights were short, and with good reason. If it took us too long to get to someone, their chances of survival were slim.

Usually our flights were to the "point of injury" or the

actual location where the patient was injured. These are our most dangerous missions because the area is less secure. However, sometimes we fly missions to forward operating bases (FOBs, pronounced like "Bob") to do a patient transfer or pick up someone who was injured on base.

Once we arrived at the location of our patient, we assess the landing situation. Then we'd have the ground team "pop smoke," or ignite a smoke grenade. This authenticates that the people below us are the group we're speaking to on the radio, so we don't get duped into landing to an ambush or enemy position. This also enables them to tell us where they want us to land. The drifting smoke gives us a wind indication, which helps us align our approach in the most energy-efficient way, that is, into the wind.

One aircraft then lands while the other provides cover from the air. The PJs jump out and go get the patient while the aircraft takes off again to allow the people on the ground to hear one another talk. When the PJs call "ready" on the radio, we go back in to pick them and the patient up. At that point, it's time to boogie out of Dodge and head to the hospital, which was called the Role 3 at Kandahar. When we arrive at the Role 3, an ambulance is usually waiting on the landing pad to take the patient to the hospital.

If we don't get called right back out, we hit the gas station before taxiing back to the ramp. Then we head into the TOC to debrief the mission with intel to discuss what went right or where we can improve. The event then concludes with the unpausing of the interrupted Xbox game.

After arriving in Kandahar, we had a few relatively straight-forward missions that let us get our feet wet. Then, a few weeks into the deployment, in May 2007, my crew and I were tasked with forward deploying to a little Dutch base connected to the town of Tarin Kowt. Forward deploying is when we spend a few weeks supporting a specific team. This was a rotation that every crew would find themselves on at some point, but not everyone looked forward to it as much as I did. I wanted to get into the action, and Tarin Kowt was definitely in the middle of the hot zone. Special Forces ODA guys were working out of "TK," as we called it, and the dangerous nature of the area and their mission necessitated having a dedicated medevac team on alert.

The rub was that we could only afford to send one crew, so you were on alert for twenty-four hours instead of the standard twelve-hour shifts in Kandahar and most other places. We did, technically, get our required crew rest, but this meant that the second we got called on a mission, our clock would start. We could fly as much as needed for the next twelve hours, but then we'd go into crew rest and they would have to task an asset from another base if needed. However, if you fly only one mission, your crew rest starts as soon as you land from the original mission. So, when you got a mission at, say, noon, you never knew if you'd be flying until midnight or flying again *starting* at midnight. Basically we were always on alert. It was exhausting, but this kind of work was the exact reason I had gotten into this business in the first place.

The upside of being at TK was that you flew fewer times a day, and the environment was extremely casual. Almost everyone on the tiny "base" was an operator, as opposed to the area being riddled with nonoperators or "non-ers" (pronounced like "Connors"), like in Kandahar. Non-ers is a derogatory term for people whose jobs don't directly impact the mission and who seem to care only about things like whether or not you were wearing your reflective belt, a safety measure often ridiculed by operators due to the fact that it makes you a target for the enemy. This is not to say that operators don't respect the people who support them. We consider most of them valued members of our team. But we'll call someone a non-er if they demonstrate a clear lack of understanding for the impact their actions have on those of us on the front lines. I suppose for some people, even in Kandahar, the greatest danger you face is getting hit by a supply truck.

TK contained a hospital and had a small US courtyard attached to it. A six-week rotation at TK had plenty of negatives, but there were some positives, too: namely the food, the sand volleyball court, and the feeling that you were truly on the front lines. The flight there was pretty amazing, too—the terrain between Kandahar and TK included a plateau with a deep, twisting ravine running through it. During this flight, we would dive toward the mouth of the creek that ran through the high ground and sort of ski our way through. We pretended that we were trying to maintain a low profile, but really, it was just a flat-out thrill to carve through the terrain this way. The flight consisted of banking left and right, bouncing the

At Tarin Kowt (TK) with MJ flying.

downward rotor wash off the walls like a snowboarder on a half-pipe.

The base at TK was surrounded by high walls topped with razor wire. Throughout the night, you'd wake to the sound of the HIMARS (High Mobility Artillery Rocket Systems) firing at militants who were positioned to attack the FOB. In addition to the hospital at the base, we had a US forward surgical team (FST). I ended up spending quite a bit of my downtime hanging out in their hospital. If I was wide-awake with nothing to do (like after landing from a mission), I'd go to the FST to see if they needed any help.

We worked hard and played hard at TK. Between the volleyball tournaments and barbecues, the grills powered by diesel fuel, we would catch some rays, play cards, and work out. When I wasn't helping out in the hospital, I spent most of my time in the gym, thoroughly enjoying the view as the ODA guys lifted weights all around me, trying my hardest not to trip on the treadmill when one of them took off his shirt.

My first combat crew was a dream team. Curt Green, who was a New York City firefighter with a great reputation and steely nerves, served as our Aircraft Commander. Curt made a perfect mentor for me on my first combat missions. Our Flight Engineer, Matt Infante, was a relatively young but somewhat seasoned guy with a great head on his shoulders. I trusted them both instantly. Thor Rasmussen, a young kid who had come from the fixed-wing world, was a great medic, and he adjusted to the fast pace and danger of the helo world quickly. The four of us hit it off immediately.

Not so much for the last member of my crew, Richard. Richard looked the part of the elderly New York Irish cop he was—pale white skin and a paintbrush mustache, a bright-red nose, and a spare tire around the middle. The first week in Kandahar, he told me straight to my face that he didn't want me on the crew.

"Nothing personal. It's just that women can't hold their own in an evasion scenario." I wondered how he'd do, lugging all that extra weight around his belly, if we needed to evade capture.

"Okay," I retorted. "Let's find out. Come on." I put down my gear and dropped into "front-leaning rest," which is the smart-ass military expression for the push-up position. "Right now . . . push-up contest," I continued from the ground. "Let's see who wins."

Throughout my career, this was my go-to rebuttal for blatant jabs at my physical ability. I had done it dozens of times, and I won every single contest I challenged someone to. That's not to say that I could out-push every guy I flew with. Hardly. But for some reason, it was never the strong, fit guys who were threatened enough by me to imply I was physically inferior. It was always the guys who were at the bottom rung of the physical fitness ladder. It was as if, like any bully, they were so insecure that they had to seek out someone they thought was weaker than they were and kick them around. I had never lost a push-up challenge like this, and I was not about to start now. I would push the ground until my arms fell off if I had to.

"Whatever," Richard harrumphed, walking away. He acted as if I was not worth the effort, but everyone knew that he was afraid he would lose. It wouldn't be the last time we would come head-to-head, but one day soon he would try to make me pay for humiliating him.

His instant dismissal of me did remind me of an important lesson, though. I thought back to the worm I'd eaten in pilot training and the instructor's advice to never write off a member of the team because of their appearance. That's just Leadership 101. I was an expert marksman who had studied the local area with the tenacity of a medical student studying anatomy. I knew some of the language and how to find water. I was certain I'd be an asset if we found ourselves in a ground fight, but there would be no convincing Richard of that fact. Another thing I'd learned over my years of training—demanding respect did nothing. I would have to earn it.

I did notice that no one came to my defense during our argument, including the Aircraft Commander I had grown to admire. I guessed I really was on my own. Curt was new to the squadron as well, having just transferred in from the unit in California. I assume it wasn't worth it to Curt to make an enemy of Richard so early on. I wasn't sure what pissed me off more—Richard's outward sexism or everyone's tacit acceptance of it.

My third day at Tarin Kowt, at around ten in the morning, I was stepping out of the shower hut after my workout. Suddenly my radio crackled: "REDCON ONE!" My walk turned to a jog across the gravel in flip-flops.

We'd had plenty of false starts, rushing to sit in the bird, the rotors turning and ready to go, only to stand down. But not this time—an American ████████ soldier had caught a bullet in the arm, and it was wheels up. I was thrilled to finally be getting my first real "rescue" of my career, even if it was only an arm injury. I gave a "Woo-hoo!" as I rounded the nose of the aircraft and jumped into my seat. I punched coordinates into the GPS, my hair still wet and dripping down under my helmet onto my heavy body armor, everything already caked with dust. Curt picked up the helo, and we stormed across the fence into enemy territory.

We'd already been airborne for half an hour when the request for blood came in over the radio. We had been slightly zigzagging our path to the landing zone so as to remain unpredictable and keep the enemy from knowing exactly where we were heading. It was the tactical way to fly, but upon hearing the request for blood, we instantly wished we had thrown the rule book out the window and beelined right to the patient. If they needed blood, the patient was in worse shape than we thought. Five more minutes and we'd already be wheels down at the pickup point. To return now for blood would take too long.

The other pilot shot me a grim look as I replied to the call.

"Just pop smoke—we're five mikes out." A bright-green plume shot up, marking the landing zone, and we landed just upwind from it.

Hardly waiting for the rotor's dust storm to clear, a ███████ ███████ soldier rushed on board with the patient in a litter. My medic told me later that he saw a look in the escort's eyes that told him he would be facing a physical confrontation if he tried to tell the patient's comrade that he couldn't come along. We weren't supposed to take anyone but the patient, but no one argued. On the stretcher, a heavily bearded sergeant breathed shallowly, his camouflage uniform half cut away. This was no arm injury.

Yes, technically the bullet had entered near the tan line of his upper arm, but it had tumbled from there and torn through his chest. These guys were the mission, the reason I came to this place—they bravely fought the enemy, always with the knowledge that medevac birds like ours were ready to scramble and get them lifesaving care in an instant.

We picked up within minutes, going airborne with bullets popping on the rocks around the landing zone below us. Thor, our medic, immediately got to work, while the other ██████ ████ soldier watched, stone-faced.

"This guy's Code Blue," I heard on the intercom. Thor was telling our crew that he had lost a pulse and the patient wasn't going to make it. I punched in the coordinates for TK, and we flew a dead-straight path, pulling every ounce of power we could out of the engines. Against regulations, we told our sister ship that we were going to have to leave them. Each aircraft is a little different. Some have stronger engines, and some are lighter. On this day, our aircraft was more powerful, and they wouldn't be able to keep up. Despite the fact that we would likely lose this patient, and splitting up put both aircraft in a lot of danger, none of us would be able to live with ourselves if we hadn't done everything possible to try to save his life.

Between checking the route, the instruments, and the systems, I stole another glance back into the cargo area behind me. Thor had straddled the patient to start CPR. The injured soldier was young and couldn't have even been thirty. There wasn't a touch of gray in the thick beard that special-ops forces grow to blend in better with the Afghan fighters. The deep tan of his face looked pale.

"We've got a pulse back!" I heard over the intercom, but we were still about fifteen minutes from the nearest medical facility, even though we were maxing out the helo's speed.

Ten minutes out, Thor started CPR again and kept it going until we landed. An ambulance on base rushed the sergeant off to surgery. We found out later that he'd lost so much blood, when they cracked his chest open to start the surgery, he didn't even bleed.

I desperately wanted this guy to live, and I knew the rest of my crew was having the exact same thought. This guy deserved to return home to the family I was certain was waiting for him.

My first patient was my first casualty. He left a tar of blood and dust an inch deep on the Pave Hawk floor. After shutting down the aircraft and getting it ready for our next mission, I walked the hundred yards across the courtyard, past the barracks, the chow hall, the gym, and the TOC to the hospital to confirm what I already knew in my heart—we had lost him. I would have known it even if I hadn't seen him lose so much blood. A palpable sense of loss hung heavy in the dust and heat all around me.

The plywood door into the FST had a painted unit badge on the outside. I yanked it open, feeling the counterweight rise on the inside, which enabled the door to swing shut on its own to keep out the flies. Inside, it was clear the staff had done all they could with the resources at their disposal, but let's just say I was highly motivated to avoid the need for surgery while at TK.

When I swung the door open, the first nurse who saw me immediately looked down at the floor. She knew why I was there, and she didn't want to have to be the one to tell me.

"How'd the surgery go?" I asked her with a waver in my voice.

"There's nothing you guys could have done," she told me

with sympathy in her eyes. "He nicked the aorta. He could have been shot on the steps of the FST and we wouldn't have been able to save him."

To this day I don't know if she was just trying to make me feel better or if it was true. Either way, I couldn't stop going over the situation again and again in my head, agonizing over where I could've shaved a few seconds off our rescue attempt, wondering if an extra precious minute or two might have saved his life.

As I walked back to the barracks, I saw one of the ODA guys kneeling in front of their memorial wall, where they meticulously painted the names of those they lost. He was dry-eyed but stone-faced, quietly painting the name of my patient onto the wall while another was lowering the flag to half-mast.

Later that night, as I headed back to my room after spending twenty minutes pushing food around on my plate at dinner, I stopped and saluted in front of the memorial wall as an ODA soldier played "Taps" on his bagpipes. The lyrics, which always brought back a welling of tears at the thought of my dad, now held an even deeper meaning for me. *Day is done, gone the sun, from the lakes, from the hills, from the sky. All is well, safely rest. God is nigh.* I was living these lyrics.

The sun was setting, and for the first time, I questioned whether or not I could really do this job. Somewhere in the US, an eight-year-old little girl had just lost her twenty-eight-year-old hero of a father. Her life would never be the same, and she didn't even know it yet.

I grew up as a pilot that day. I would never wish for a mission again.

———— ● ————

The rotation at TK was rough. Even when we thought we had done some good, things could go bad very quickly. One night we were called out on a mission and assigned a two-Apache escort. That was never a good sign—it meant that we were going into a particularly dangerous area. On that night, we were headed into the heart of bad-guy territory to pick up a wounded three-year-old out of an unfriendly village. Intel reported that the three-year-old was in need of medevac due to chemical burns he had sustained inhaling fumes from his father's homemade fertilizer bomb.

As we landed, I surveyed the town in my night-vision goggles. About fifty yards away from us, people began to emerge and cluster together, pointing and gesturing at us. The small crowd began walking our way and suddenly grew to a group of about thirty people jogging toward us. This didn't look good. I called it in to the Apaches overhead and started checking to see if anyone in the group was armed. How close could we let them get before we would have to take off?

When they were about twenty-five yards away, Curt slightly lifted the collective, ready to pull pitch and get us out of there. Just then the beautiful attack helicopters that were with us flew a low pass about fifteen feet off of the ground, right off our nose. The message to the growing crowd was clear: *That's close enough.* The townspeople screeched to a halt, continuing to stand there and wave a fist now and then, but we were able to load our patient and get out safely. *Didn't they know we were trying to save one of their kids?*

The boy's father boarded the aircraft alongside his son but wouldn't speak to us. He just glared at us with his sun-darkened, wrinkled eyes. It was as if he expected us to try to kill them both at any minute. The little boy, on the other hand, quickly stole our hearts. We could see that he was in pain and utterly terrified. The sound of the helicopter was probably the loudest, most frightening thing he had ever experienced, and Thor, who was checking his vitals, was clearly scaring him. It was at that time my medic won my loyalty forever.

I had never really noticed, but apparently, Thor carried a Beanie Baby–sized teddy bear on his vest for times just like this. When he pulled it from its pouch and then lifted the boy's hand to place the bear on his chest, the little boy's fear disappeared. The smile that briefly crossed his face before he snuggled into the teddy bear was the type of moment that reminded us why we were over there.

After we got him back to the base and into the hospital, I couldn't seem to get him out of my mind. I kept going back to visit this little angel, as I often did my other patients, to see how he was doing. Each day he looked a little better. On the third day, I came in to see him, but he wasn't there. I was disappointed not to see him but was so happy that he had recovered enough to go home. One of the nurses who knew me walked over to me as I smiled down at his empty bed.

"I'm so sorry. I guess it was just too much for his little lungs."

He hadn't gotten better—he had contracted pneumonia and died the previous night. I walked out trying to convince myself that it was okay, that he had died peacefully, but no matter how I painted it in my mind, to this day I cry for that sweet casualty of this terrible war.

———— • ————

Soon enough we were replaced by another crew for their six-week rotation, and we returned to Kandahar. While we hated being back under the microscope of the brass and other "non-ers," being at Kandahar Airfield (KAF) did have its benefits. Since we would once again be working only twelve-hour shifts with a twelve-hour break, we could count on a good night's sleep (if one of our eight roommates didn't leave their damn alarm on). We also were happy about getting a decent cup of coffee at the Canadian Tim Hortons.

The lodging at KAF was sort of like long double-wides. The cement-floored rooms contained four bunk beds, eight particle-board wardrobes with a couple of drawers in them, and no windows. But with a little ingenuity, you could make the bare-bones lodging quite comfortable.

I bought a great Afghan rug for a hundred dollars to cover up the cement, hung up a sheet for some privacy, then strung a few Christmas lights overhead to get some light without bothering those nearby who were on opposite shifts. I ordered groceries online from a website that would mail me nonperishables like powdered milk, which I would mix up to pour over the cereal I always grabbed from the chow hall. The chow hall was all juice, soda, and water. Milk was, oddly enough, one of the things I missed most from home.

KAF was also fun because of all the different people we could interact with there. I was particularly close to our Army comrades. We often flew escort for the unarmed Dustoff guys. These are the crews whose primary mission is medevac. The Red Cross on the tail of their aircraft demanded that they be unarmed, but this didn't matter to our enemies. They would kill someone trying to save a life (often an Afghan life) just as quickly as they would someone shooting at them. Between missions, I really enjoyed getting to know the Dustoff crews. Their tactics differed from ours tremendously, and I felt like it made me a better wingman to understand how they flew so that I could predict their actions better during a mission.

While on shift at the TOC, there was a litany of things to do with ourselves to pass time between missions. While I certainly played my share of Xbox, one of the things I enjoyed most was double-checking my gear and cleaning my rifle. It was a ritual at the start of each shift to go to my locker and ensure that everything was right where it should be. But on one particular shift, I was in for a surprise. Ammo was tightly controlled, and for good reason. You had to answer to your chain of command anytime you fired your weapon, and every round was carefully tracked and counted. That day I stared dumbfounded into my locker until it finally soaked in. I was clearly missing a magazine of 9mm ammo for my handgun.

But that was impossible. No one was more careful about their gear than I was—no one.

I started tearing apart my locker, looking for it, refusing to accept the fact that it was missing. I turned out every pocket, emptied every bag, and desperately ran my fingers along the edges of the locker. I must have searched for twenty minutes. Then I heard a chuckle behind me that raised the hairs on the back of my neck.

"Lose something?"

It was the guy who told me he didn't want to fly with me because I was a woman: Richard. He was leaning against the lockers across from mine, eating a Ding Dong. He shook his head and gave a short chuckle as he walked away. I felt in my gut in that instant that he had taken it and there would be no finding it now. Furious, I made sure my radio was turned on, the volume high enough to hear a REDCON call, and I stormed out of the TOC. I found myself walking down the taxiway, my heart pounding, my stomach in knots. Being around the aircraft usually reminded me why I was here and kept me from going crazy, but this time, nothing helped. I was still livid. Then I looked up and saw the lights on in the Army TOC, so I decided to pay them a visit. I could use some friendly faces, and unfortunately, I already knew from experience that none of the guys in my squadron would take my side against Richard.

Luckily for me, a few of the pilots I had gotten to know were hanging out and greeted me with cheery salutations. In that low moment, it felt really good to be treated like I belonged. I'd been hanging out with them for about an hour and was starting to feel a little less angry when one of them pulled me aside and asked me what was wrong. He could tell I wasn't myself. I couldn't help it—I relayed to him the whole story, half expecting him to report me for the missing ammo.

"Who cares what one old fart thinks?" he asked.

"No, it's more than that. I'm going to get my ass handed to me over the missing ammo," I replied. "I guess I better just go report it missing and get it over with."

"Oh, is that what's bothering you? Here, I have an extra mag," he said, and handed one over without hesitation.

I stood there staring at my salvation resting in my palm. I sputtered a "thank you" and stared up at him.

"Don't worry." He laughed, noting the disbelieving look on my face. "I can get more."

I couldn't believe it. Clearly things were different in the Army, and it made me realize how ridiculous some of our Air Force rules were. I felt a knot loosen in my chest. I threw my arms around him in an uncharacteristic hug, and he just laughed and patted my shoulder. My relief was almost overwhelming. From that moment on, I never let my ammunition out of my sight again—I took it with me everywhere I went.

I walked back to my TOC and slipped the spare mag into my vest in my locker. Just then I started to worry. I couldn't pretend I had never lost the magazine; above all, I prided myself on my integrity. But mere minutes later, I happened to overhear Richard tattling on me for the missing ammo. Before I could even turn around, my commander stalked into the room with Richard on his heels.

"Jennings," he barked. "Can you account for your ammo?"

I looked Richard square in the eye. "Yes, sir, I can," I told him.

"Bullsh*t," Richard said.

"Show me," my commander instructed, a tired edge to his voice. I think he had seen this particular prank before, and he had better things to do with his time.

"Here you go." I waved my arm like Vanna White at my vest hanging in my locker. He counted and turned to Richard.

"She's good to go. Anything else?"

Richard just stormed off without answering. My commander shook his head and started to walk back to the desk he occupied.

"Um, sir?" I said to his back.

He turned around. "That's all I needed, MJ."

"Right, but I have to tell you—" I started to say, but he just raised a hand and cut me off. I could see in his face that he knew exactly what had happened.

"No, you really don't. You're good to go, and that's all I need to know. Hang in there, MJ. You're doing a great job."

Over the weeks that followed, rumors circulated about the incident that were even more painful than the moment itself. A friend reported to me that Richard started telling people about my "lost" magazine and that he happened to have it on good authority that I had lost it "out by the fence."

When this rumor was relayed to me by a fellow pilot, I was confused. Did he mean I'd lost my ammo while I was jogging the perimeter? The pilot shook his head uncomfortably and explained to me that Richard was insinuating I'd been performing oral sex and must have dropped it.

My stomach roiled, and I felt like throwing up. I had been so careful since arriving in Kandahar to stay above this sort of thing. I hadn't so much as flirted with any aircrew members precisely to avoid being made into such a joke. My behavior thus far was above reproach, and now this guy was spreading rumors all over the squadron about me just because I had foiled his plot and made him look like an ass instead of the other way around? I couldn't believe it.

Back at the barracks, I was telling a friend about it in the bathroom we all shared. One of the other girls overheard us and chimed in.

"But I don't see what the big deal is. It isn't true, so why do you care?" I just shook my head. This particular girl had a different standard of behavior than I did and epitomized everything I was trying to avoid. Of course she wouldn't understand.

I tried to explain to her that it wasn't the fact that he had lied about the sexual act that was bothering me. It was the fact that Richard and the others didn't see me as a strong, competent, well-trained pilot who deserved his respect. Just because my anatomy was different from his, he had to objectify and sexualize me. He had to paint me in a role subservient to him and his fellow men, and what was worse, they had gone along with it. I could no longer pretend he was the only one who felt that way just because he was the only one who was dumb enough to actually say it out loud. Enough of them had been entertained by his gossip that the rumor had made it all the way back to me.

I was furious and decided I wouldn't stand for this treatment. I wasn't trying to demand their respect. I had earned their respect, dammit. It was obvious that I was never going to fit in with this unit. About half of the guys were really awesome, and I would love to fly with them again someday. But that other half, the ones who defined their masculinity by the job they did, were obviously threatened by the fact that I was just as good at my job as they were. After all, if this job made them a man, and a woman did it just as well or better than them, what did that mean for them?

———— • ————

Over the next few weeks I found myself spending more and more time alone. It was an entirely self-imposed isolation. I withdrew from the people around me, no longer knowing who my real friends were. I would have taken a bullet for any one of those guys, but many of them apparently didn't feel the same way. They just wanted me to disappear.

Outside the TOC, there were a few cargo bins, like the ones you'd see stacked up at shipping docks, where we kept various pieces of equipment and supplies. Someone had built a gazebo on top of one along with a rickety staircase that led up to it. Not a lot of people hung out up there, partly due to the smell of the nearby "sh*t pond." The base's sewage was sent there, and we joked daily about the lovely smell of

Kandahar. In a stroke of brilliant engineering, the flightline area was positioned directly downwind of the sh*t pond. But to be honest, I preferred it to the stench of male chauvinism given off by some of my fellow airmen.

The Christmas lights on the gazebo emitted a colorful, soft glow, and I would usually just enjoy the solitude watching the sun set while smoking a good cigar. Occasionally someone would come up to join me and chitchat, but I wasn't much for conversation those days.

About halfway through the deployment, at one of my lowest moments, I was leaning on the railing, looking out over the flightline at night, when I heard heavy boots stomping up the unsteady stairs. I didn't know who it was, and I didn't care.

"What the f**k is this?" I heard an unfamiliar voice declare, and I turned to see a new face.

"Hi," I said, not offering my name or my hand. I had grown untrusting over the last few months.

He didn't seem to notice. "Hi. I'm Steve."

I shook his outstretched hand and said, "MJ."

"Good to meet you," he said. "Now what the f**k is this?" he asked, looking around at the view.

I couldn't help but chuckle. Over the next twenty minutes or so, I ruminated with him about the glory of the gazebo and the lovely stench coming from the sh*t pond. Then I gave him the lay of the land at KAF, and he told me a little bit about himself.

He was part of a unit from California that had just arrived to do their rotation in the TOC next to ours. We would continue doing medevac while they pulled the CSAR alert. I didn't know it then, but Steve Burt, a Flight Engineer from Oregon who served the 129th Rescue Squadron in the California Air National Guard, would eventually become one of my closest friends.

Steve was soon joined by other members of his unit, and within minutes I felt my mood lift. These guys instantly welcomed me, happy for the intel I was giving them about where to get the best coffee and how to order cigars. It wasn't long before we were laughing and kicking back.

Then my radio crackled, and I grabbed it off of my belt as I dashed for the stairs, handing Steve my cigar as I ran past him.

"REDCON ONE," I heard blaring from all the radios scattered around the area as I jogged off.

"Have fun!" Steve called after me, raising my cigar in salute. My mind was on the mission at hand, but there was certainly a little more pep in my step as I headed out to the aircraft and spun her up, ready for the next trip across the fence. I knew in my heart that I had found my people, and I couldn't wait to hang out with them again.

A couple of weeks later, my first impression of these guys was cemented. It was July Fourth, and apparently, they felt like celebrating. A bunch of their guys transformed themselves into walking wounded by covering themselves with gauze and Ace bandages. They marched down the flightline beating a makeshift drum, then entered the British hangar, to the astonishment of our allies inside.

The California commander approached the British commander, lightly slapped her across the face with a glove, and challenged her and her unit to a water-gun battle for colonial independence. Preparations were made, and a giant water gun and balloon war ensued. I watched from the sidelines as others from my unit grumbled their disapproval, but I looked on, glassy-eyed—wishing I were part of their team.

Over the next couple of months, I spent a lot of time next door to my own TOC in the CSAR building, hanging out with the guys from California. We would hit chow together, play basketball or work out together, and kick one another's butts at Halo. This fantastic group of men and women were laid-back in attitude but tight when it came to the things that mattered, somehow easygoing while simultaneously maintaining very high standards. They were quick to laugh and treated each other like family. I knew my unit resented my hanging out with them, but I honestly couldn't have cared less.

———— ◈ ————

Within a few weeks, when it came time for my unit to go home, we all had thoughts of family, cheeseburgers, beer, and clean air at the forefront of our minds, but to be honest, I was in no rush to go back stateside with my unit. While I considered a few of them to be friends, I'd had just about enough of the rest of them and their sh*tty attitudes.

As it happened, I had heard that one of the pilots from the unit coming in to replace us had a wife who was about to have a baby. I had been looking for an opportunity to keep racking up my combat hours, and since I was more than happy to stick around with my new buds from the California unit, I decided to volunteer to augment the incoming unit. I would pull my second tour in Afghanistan without ever going back home.

My unit thought I was crazy, but I waved goodbye to them happily as they boarded their plane. I would never have chosen to stick around with those guys, but I was really looking forward to staying to get to know my new, temporary unit. Whoever they were, I doubted they'd be as cool as the folks from California. But I also knew they couldn't be as bad as some of the people I'd flown with from New York.

Lucky for me, my new unit, the 33rd Rescue Squadron from Kadena, Japan, was another awesome group of folks. I was truly excited to be flying with them. Some of them had been to Kandahar before, since the active-duty folks deployed a lot more frequently than us Guard people.

Right off the bat, they crewed me with a seasoned Flight Engineer and Gunner but an inexperienced Aircraft Commander. The AC was a young guy named Mike who was being groomed for Weapons School. Weapons School was like our version of Top Gun, where the best of the best would go to train. I was excited to see what I could learn from him.

As it turned out, though, flying with this guy would be no learning experience. Mike would yank and bank the aircraft into aggressive attitudes (the position of the aircraft relative to the ground), frequently putting his crew in danger.

More than once I expressed the opinion to him that, should we take a round of fire to anything critical on the aircraft, many of the situations he was putting us into would be unrecoverable. I was sure he was just excited to finally be flying in combat, but I had quite a few combat hours under my belt already, and I had learned the hard way that this wasn't something to be excited about. He needed to learn to respect the environment and the fact that the enemy was hiding behind every rock.

On a hot afternoon in August of 2007, I was flying with Mike, and we were shooting an approach into Bagram Airfield. I was on the controls but was unable to slow the aircraft down enough to avoid passing our lead aircraft. So I decided that the safest thing would be to execute a "go-around." In our line of work, it's common to say that "go-arounds are free." This means that anyone should at any time feel free to call a go-around if you feel the aircraft is unsafe. In Mike's defense, it sucks to do a go-around on an airfield. You have the chance of messing up the flow of air traffic, and it makes you look bad to the tower. But sending your aircraft and crew into a crater on the ground looks far worse.

Just as I began my go-around, Mike yanked the controls away from me. He banked hard left, and we swooped behind our lead aircraft, barely missing their tail rotor with our refueling probe. Seeing this, I instantly braced myself for a crash. His crazy zigzag maneuver had slowed us down enough to avoid executing a go-around, but that hardly seemed worth it as the entire crew gasped, all of us probably expecting to die.

Only when it appeared that we'd be able to land safely did I start breathing again. There was an uncharacteristic silence on the radio. No one said a word. As the Co-Pilot, I was responsible for shutting the aircraft engines and systems down. But instead of taking care of the checklist items, I just unstrapped and got out of the aircraft as fast as I could. Mike took the hint and completed the checklist as I walked away with my helmet in my hand.

Luckily for me, there was another crew on the deck waiting for the aircraft, and they had seen the whole thing. Thank goodness, because *no one* would have to take my word for what had just happened—it would have sounded completely insane.

"What the hell was that? Are you guys okay?" demanded the commander and the squadron safety officer who stopped me on the deck.

All of the color had drained out of my face, and I just shook my head and kept walking. My commander followed me, so I had to do my best to piece together what had happened. I told him that I would never get into another aircraft with that cowboy again because I didn't want to die.

My commander totally understood, apologizing to me for the whole experience, and immediately assigned me to a new crew. It seemed to me he felt some sort of responsibility for trying and failing to control Mike, who seemed to be some sort of golden boy who was being protected by someone high up in the chain of command. This lack of impartiality, I had discovered, was insidious in the military. Ultramasculine guys who fly the same way they live their lives—too hard, too fast, too careless—are often depicted as the perfect combat warriors. Instead, they usually end up undermining the mission, as their teams cannot depend on them to make the best decisions under pressure.

Years later, I was heartbroken to hear that Mike had been piloting an aircraft in Afghanistan that took enemy fire and crashed. He and most of his crew died in the crash, and the two who survived were severely disabled.

Nearing the end of my deployment in 2007, I was walking from the aircraft to the TOC, carrying my gear in at the end of my shift, when I heard a familiar voice. No f**king way. I stopped dead in my tracks and looked around until I saw him.

"ZERK?" I almost didn't believe it, and by the look on his face, neither did he. The Air Force is a small world, and Rescue is even smaller, so it wasn't uncommon to bump into your buddies. But here in the middle of the hot Afghan desert? It just seemed like fate kept bringing us back together. I was so happy to see him.

"Holy sh*t! What up, MJ?"

I dropped my gear and gave Keenan a quick hug. I knew I wouldn't get to see him much, as we were flying different missions and I'd be at TK a lot, but it was really great to see him again. I held to a steadfast rule of not dating the guys I flew with, and although I sometimes regretted it (especially around Zerk), it had served me well. I wouldn't break my rule for him, though it was tempting. I would see him now and then in passing, but we were always running to answer the radios or sit in on a briefing.

I was also busy getting to know the new crew I'd been assigned to. I was relieved—already it seemed like it was going to be a much better fit. I was excited to learn that my new Aircraft Commander was one of our most senior pilots. He was serving as the second-in-command, and I felt much safer flying with him. Despite my combat hours, I was still a relatively new pilot, so I was eager to learn from him. He would soon teach me one of the best lessons of my career. Unfortunately for him, it would be at his own expense.

One day, a few months into my second deployment, we were launching on a mission just like any other, with our usual high sense of urgency but also with a strict adherence to protocol. My AC was on the controls, taxiing us out, when the TOC relayed updated coordinates for our pickup. I had noticed that there was a fire truck parked on the taxiway, but that was hardly rare, so I called it out to him and he acknowledged it as I went "heads in" and looked down at the navigation system to update our coordinates. As a partnership, the two pilots take turns flying and operating the systems. When one pilot has their hands on the controls, they are "heads out" and looking outside the aircraft. The other can go "heads in" at times to navigate, adjust radios, or check systems.

The next thing I knew, I heard a loud thumping and felt the aircraft lurch to the right. We had hit the fire truck with our rotors. Technically this would go down as "his fault," given the fact that he was the Aircraft Commander and the one driving the bird, but I would forever remember this as my greatest failure as a pilot. I should never have assumed he was so senior that he didn't need me backing him up. I had failed him by trusting that he didn't need my help. I should have waited until we were clear of the truck before punching in the coordinates, and I learned a huge lesson that day about human fallibility. No one is above making mistakes. While I thought I was showing him respect by trusting him to clear the vehicle, the reality is that it was my failure, too.

To this day I regret this incident, but I have to wonder what bigger catastrophes I was able to avoid due to the fact that I learned that important lesson when I did. We were close to the end of the deployment already, and that mission would complete my tour that year. The required investigation that would clear me to fly again after the incident would take longer than we had left in our deployment. So within days of the accident, I said farewell to KAF and headed home.

I had a few weeks of leave coming to me, so I decided to spend some time in Austin, as I had no desire to go see my "friends" in New York. The people who had brought me to the New York unit had either retired or passed away, and I was a little unsure of who was left. I knew that the majority of them had no problem with my being a woman, but they also hadn't stood up for me; nor had they stopped the discrimination I was suffering at the hands of the few in Kandahar who did. Most of them had played a role, some large, some small, in one of the lowest moments in my career thus far. Yes, they had sent me to pilot training, so I felt I owed them a debt, but I was in no rush to go back and pay it off.

A few days into my leave in Austin, my phone rang. It was from a California area code, so I jumped to answer it, hoping it would be my new friends from Kandahar. Sure enough, it was the unit from California. Better yet, they had great news for me.

Knowing how unhappy I was with my unit, they had found me a job working for the California Counterdrug Task Force, part of the Air National Guard unit. I would be a member of the 129th Rescue Squadron while also flying marijuana-eradication missions.

I was beyond thrilled, but I hesitated, because part of me still felt I owed New York, despite everything some of them had put me through. Then the commander explained to me that earlier that year they had sent Curt—the Aircraft Commander I'd flown with during my deployment—to New York, so getting a Co-Pilot in return was a fair swap. I couldn't believe my luck.

My head instantly filled with visions of wine tasting, surfing, and all-around great California dreams. Within a few weeks of the phone call, I had packed up my car with all of my belongings and gotten on the road. This time around at the crossroads, I would head west.

SIX

REPORTING TO THE 129th Rescue Squadron at Moffett Federal Airfield in Silicon Valley was the beginning of the happiest part of my entire career. I was worried that I'd be bored flying stateside missions after two back-to-back tours in Afghanistan, but I couldn't have been more wrong. Flying with this unit was everything I had ever hoped for as a rescue pilot.

I was one of three pilots assigned to the elite Counterdrug Task Force flying unit named Team Hawk. On my first day of work, I walked into the Team Hawk room, and the first person I saw was a burly guy who was concentrating so hard it looked like he was going to bite his tongue off, pecking the computer keyboard in what only distantly seemed like an attempt at typing. He looked up and broke out into a huge grin that matched mine. It was Steve Burt, my cigar-smoking buddy from KAF.

"Well, holy sh*t. Look what the cat dragged in. How the f**k are *you*?" Steve asked as he got up to give me a shoulder-slapping hug. I breathed a huge sigh of relief—I was back with my people. I greeted the other two pilots, who had also become friends of mine in Afghanistan. Something in my chest untied—I'd found my home.

One of the other two pilots was my new boss. Finn was the Team Hawk Commander and a huge part of why I was in California in the first place. He and I had become great friends in Afghanistan, and it was ultimately his decision to hire me. Finn was the perfect example of a clean-cut all-American pilot. He was a good ol' Midwestern boy who had graduated from the Air Force Academy and was married to a teacher. To me, he always looked the way I imagined Ender from *Ender's Game* all grown up. He had a quiet demeanor and wasn't a huge guy, but his fiery Irish side would come out now and then when he was really spun up about something. I wouldn't be surprised if someday he ends up a senator from the Buckeye state of Ohio.

The third Team Hawk pilot was Dave. Over the years, Dave and I would become close friends, and I could always rely on his loyalty and sound judgment. He and I didn't always agree on tactics, but he was a good pilot and a great friend.

After visiting my new team, I ventured out into the rest of the squadron to see who else I could bump into. One of the first people I saw was another good friend I'd made at KAF. He hailed me warmly and asked me to take a walk with him to the admin building. I could tell he wanted to talk to me in private.

"So, I just wanted to give you a heads-up because I know

what you faced in New York," he began in an ominous voice. "You'll find ninety-nine percent of the people here are thrilled to have you. You have a great reputation in rescue for being a good stick and a mission hacker."

A mission hacker is someone who relentlessly hits the mission, volunteers for the difficult flights, focuses on their career, and won't hesitate to jump out in front when the bullets start flying. It's a great compliment to a pilot, and I took it as such while also bracing for the "but" that would inevitably follow.

"But one of the guys here did fight hiring you," he continued. "He doesn't think women should be on our crews, and you're going to have an uphill battle convincing him otherwise. I debated whether or not to even tell you, but I think you should know. Hell, I think he'd tell you to your face if you asked him. His name is Doug Sherry, and he's a former Army pilot."

As it turned out, I already knew Doug, and it didn't surprise me in the slightest. All in all, he was actually a well-respected, reasonably decent guy. He wasn't your run-of-the-mill chauvinist—in other words, he didn't seem to hold a low opinion of women based on his own insecurities, and he didn't shove it in people's faces. Maybe he'd had some sort of experience with a mediocre fellow soldier on which he based his opinion, but that wasn't enough to scare me off. I actually looked forward to showing him what I could do.

One thing I did know was that, first and foremost, Doug was a damn good pilot. And I figured that once he saw that I was an asset to the team, he'd probably come around. I thanked my friend for the intel, though—it was good to know that he'd fought the decision to bring me on board. I'd have to be very careful about trusting Doug.

I certainly wouldn't be able to avoid him—he was always around. Doug walked around everywhere with an unlit, disgustingly wet stub of a cigar in his mouth, as if he had just walked off the set of *Hogan's Heroes*. He'd make crude jokes as he swapped his cigar to the other side of his mouth, coining new insults on a daily basis. "That guy's a total doucher," he'd drawl, inventing new words as he went. He was quite a character. Despite our differences, though, I can say that the unit was better off for having him on the team. Things just wouldn't be the same around there without him.

Of course, as I was running around processing into the unit that first day, I bumped right into him.

"Hi, Doug!" I said, muffling my discomfort and painting on a cheery face.

"MJ." He nodded to me. "Welcome to Moffett. Don't f**k up."

It was actually more than I had hoped for from him. After all, it was solid advice. *Don't f**k up.* I managed to convince myself that his statement was coming from a place of genuine concern for my success and well-being. Maybe.

I'd only just arrived in California, but we had to hit the ground running at Team Hawk. I jumped right into our counterdrug operations, which meant that we flew a variety of different missions. On marijuana-eradication missions, we pulled cargo nets full of marijuana plants out of the national forests. We also supported the ground forces or local law enforcement on their missions, and we occasionally even landed our helicopters at schools to show kids that staying off drugs could be "cool." We laughingly called those our "Hugs Not Drugs" missions. I do think we reached some of the kids, but most of them seemed to only want to hear about whether or not we were armed and if we had ever killed anyone.

One of my favorite Gunners to fly with was TieJie Jones. His first name was pronounced "TJ," and he was a seasoned Gunner who was a valuable member of our squadron. TJ hailed from somewhere in the Virgin Islands. He had the muscular build of a warrior but the demeanor of a retired gunslinger living the good life on a beachfront property somewhere.

Those of us who flew with the 129th during the summer of 2008 would always remember our time there. The operational tempo that summer was insane. We jumped from one thing to the next, starting with a planned Counterdrug Task Force operation called Operation LOCCUST, which stood for Locating Organized Cannabis Cultivators Using Saturation Techniques. It was a huge, multiorganizational campaign, ultimately resulting in thirty-six arrests and more than $1.4 million of cannabis eradicated, and it required us to fly out of Ukiah in the heart of marijuana country. The locals didn't bother masking their disdain for us, knowing that we were out there depleting their supply and raising their prices.

Once, we were sitting in the grass behind the shut-down,

parked helicopter, just relaxing between missions as the fuel truck was getting us ready to go back out, when we heard the loud, incessant honking of a car horn. I turned to look and saw a truck full of hippies flipping us off and shaking their fists at us. I chuckled and shook my head. Like the vast majority of my colleagues, I had never tried pot before, due in large part to the fact that we were regularly and randomly drug tested. We all knew that would be an exceedingly stupid way to end a career and flush all of our hard work down the toilet, but I'm sure I wasn't the only one curious about the lifestyle.

Our work for Operation LOCCUST was thrilling but extremely grueling. We constantly maxed out the time we were allowed to fly, and we kept our downtime to the absolute minimum required by regulation. The commander even occasionally approved extended hours, which was not something they did lightly. If there had been any mishaps, the investigation board would have jumped down his throat for approving the overtime. But we were professionals, and we had all lived through a number of brutal and difficult situations in our careers thus far. We just bonded even more closely and collectively enjoyed the suck. A cold beer and great camaraderie at the end of the day usually made up for the heat exhaustion and the unforgiving pain in our backs from twelve hours in the vibrating, rattling aircraft.

———— ◆ ————

Toward the end of the two-month operation, we were all looking forward to the upcoming break that most of us planned to spend back at home. At the time, California was experiencing one of the worst wildfire seasons in recent memory, so before we were able to leave, we were immediately retasked with helping the local firefighters protect homes and forests from the devastating destruction of the blazing infernos. We'd be fighting to protect the same forest out of which we had just been pulling marijuana.

Flying through wildfires was an incredible ordeal, almost like navigating through a terrible storm. The smoke was so thick, we couldn't rely on vision alone to navigate. In order to be able to see each other in the choking cloud, our maintenance crews marked up our camouflaged helicopters with hot-pink and neon-orange paint. It was quite a sight to see our tough-as-nails, war-fighting machines covered in hot-pink candy-cane stripes up the refueling probe, along with a three-foot-tall pink "J94" painted on our belly and tail to signify our call sign, Jolly 94.

For large operations such as LOCCUST and wildfire suppression, we would augment our core Team Hawk crew with aircrew from the rest of the squadron. My crew included Rhys Hunt, who was my Aircraft Commander and our squadron's director of operations, the second-in-command behind our squadron commander. Steve was our Flight Engineer, and Matt Rymer was our very experienced Gunner. Matt's call sign was "Blue," as in "You're my boy, Blue!" from the movie *Old School*, and he was an easygoing, smart dude who was always quick to smile.

The four of us had flown together on LOCCUST missions,

Fighting fires.

and we were kept together as a crew as we were rolled into the wildfire-suppression undertaking. The locals, it appeared, were just as mad at us on these missions, despite the fact that this time, we were trying to *save* their crops, not to mention their houses.

The way the wildfire-suppression flights work is that firefighters on the ground tell us where they want us to drop water. Usually this means we fly through smoke and toast our butts a bit in the heat in order to drop water next to an active fire to help them keep it from spreading. We had to find the water ourselves somewhere, so we were authorized to "dip" from any water source we could find. This often meant ponds on private property and, in this area in particular, ponds that fed irrigation pumps for (you guessed it) cannabis fields.

Rhys was an excellent Aircraft Commander. Instead of doing everything himself, he knew he had a young Co-Pilot next to him who was eager for experience. One day, as unnerving as I'm sure it was for him, he let me take the controls while we were filling our water bucket. The bucket was a two-hundred-gallon, parachute-like neon-orange assembly that attached to the cargo hook on the belly of the helicopter.

As I flew the helicopter over the water source, I could hear the backenders calling out, "Twenty feet . . . fifteen . . . ten . . . five, four, three, two, hold . . . filling . . . hold . . . hold . . . okay, start back up." At this point, I started to slowly lift the bird up, so that the bucket would open and fill with water as we climbed. This is a rather delicate operation. You're asking a lot of your engines to lift this much extra weight, and at the higher elevations that can be a recipe for disaster. In the event of an emergency or a power loss, both pilots are ready to hit the dump switch, which releases all of the water out of the bottom center of the bucket. With all of this at the forefront of his mind, Rhys was carefully guarding the controls as I was "on the dip," as we called it.

"Who the f**k is this guy? Twelve o'clock," Steve called out as I breathed evenly, trying to hold a perfectly stable hover and slow climb while keeping all parts of the aircraft out of the water. If I crept forward, I'd have to correct backward, which would put the tail lower than the nose. It was incredibly dangerous if you weren't holding a very solid hover. I flicked a glance out of the front of the aircraft to see an angry, bearded middle-aged man on a quad bike yelling at us from a small hill about ten feet above the water level. This put him pretty much eye-to-eye with us, so a sense of unease began to permeate the cabin. Either he was mad that we, at some point, had confiscated his weed, or he was pissed that we were taking his water in the middle of a drought. Either way, it wasn't a good situation. He could throw something at us and possibly hit a rotor, and we'd end up drowning in this twenty-foot-deep sh*t hole all because we were trying to save his house. Hell, even worse, he could shoot at us, and we'd have absolutely no way to defend ourselves.

"Okay, that's it. You're clear," Blue said over the intercom. He didn't need to tell me twice. This was music to my ears, as I couldn't wait to get away from this lunatic.

"Transitioning forward," I announced as I slowly pushed the stick forward and pulled up the collective stick to my left to give the engines the power to go from a hover to forward flight. Unfortunately, the lunatic was directly in our takeoff lane, as the trees around us precluded a different track. We'd have to fly right over him, which was less than ideal.

"Oh sh*t. Water's away," Blue reported with a chuckle. I quickly glanced over at Rhys. He had an expression of "uh-oh" on his face. I looked down. Someone must have accidentally tripped the bucket dump switch, because the guy on the quad had just gotten a two-hundred-gallon bath.

"Ha! Got you, you f**ker!" Steve shouted to uproarious laughter erupting from both Blue and Steve.

Rhys looked down at the collective he had carefully been guarding. His thumb had accidentally hit the switch during the climb.

"Um . . . ," he began. "Yeah, let's go find another dip."

We all had a good chuckle and began looking for a different pond. I kept flying. It was okay with me. The guy had looked like he needed to cool off.

With a new bucketful of water, we flew back into the action. We stayed just high enough above the flames to prevent damage to the aircraft, but it wasn't uncommon to get a bit overheated after twelve hours spent roasting like a marshmallow over a campfire. We were careful not to get too close, but sometimes we pushed it. That day, we were flying as low as we safely could en route to our spot (chosen for us by the firefighters on the ground), when we saw a large tree on fire on a hill to our left. I don't know if everything around it had burned down or if it had always been taller, but the seventy-foot tree stood at least thirty feet above everything around it, and it was completely engulfed in flames.

As we passed it out the left door, we got a little too close, and I could feel the skin at the nape of my neck start to sting like a bad sunburn. I was surprised that Blue hadn't said anything behind me, but about three seconds later, he started coughing loudly.

"Okay, that was too close," he blurted out. "I inhaled so

much heat that I couldn't breathe or talk there for a minute. I thought my visor was going to melt!"

Rhys glanced at me as he continued flying straight ahead. We weren't used to the effect on the aircraft and crew of flying to the side of the fire. We had been concentrating on flying high enough *above* it.

"Yeah, let's not do that again," he said.

At the end of each day, we all smelled like chain-smokers and suffered from heat exhaustion. The trip from the aircraft to our motel was usually pretty quiet, as half of the crew ended up dozing off, exhausted. Sometimes we'd hit a drive-through on the way back, but usually we all just wanted a shower and a decent night of sleep.

<hr />

About three days into the firefighting, we started having a lot more fun. We were becoming firefighting pros. We had no idea how long we'd be there, so we had to make the best of it. Before long, we felt like we could identify different areas of the forest by the look and smell of the smoke, as each unique type of tree burned differently.

"Wow!" I exclaimed one morning as we began our first trip into the cloud of smoke. "This smells like crap. I hope we're not over a trash site."

"I hope there aren't any animals down there," Rhys added. "It sort of smells like a skunk."

"Great," Steve piped in. "That'll really help me score with the front-desk chick."

"Oh, sure, Steve," I said, laughing. "It's the smoke smell that's keeping you from getting laid. Whatever you need to tell yourself." I could never resist giving Steve good-natured sh*t.

We all laughed, and the intellect of the day pretty much went downhill from there as we traded jabs and laughed at one another. We even started giving the other pilots on our radio frequency sh*t when they would hit bingo fuel before us and have to return to the airport for more gas. This was ridiculous, as we all knew, because your skill doesn't determine your fuel flow, but it was good-natured ribbing about having the guts to squeeze one more dip out of your empty fuel tanks. We may have even pushed it a little too much ourselves, flying until we were running on fumes as well. Eventually our fun day came to an end, and it was time to drive back to the motel. On the drive home, Blue pointed out a diner on our normal route, and despite our exhaustion, we all jumped at the chance to stop and grab a bite to eat before returning to the motel.

It was during this meal that I began feeling like maybe the heat exhaustion was getting to us. Everyone was laughing that sort of uncontrollable giggling you get when you've been up too long or working out in the sun too much. We devoured our dinner and ordered more food, eyeing the pies in the glass display case. I'm not sure who started it, but then we began texting other crews, trying to see who would come and join the party. We were having way too good a time to just call it a night.

Eventually, Rhys thought it would be funny to start texting

our Squadron Commander. No one seemed to realize that this wasn't a great idea, given that it was ten o'clock at night. We all started ribbing him just as hard as we'd been doing among our crew all day. Then he hit us with a sobering response.

I glanced down at my phone when my text notification *ding*ed, and what I read just about made me lose my dinner. I locked eyes with Rhys across the table and realized he had gotten the same text.

Are you guys high? the text said. *I think we're going to have to test your whole crew when we get back.*

We looked at each other for about three seconds in terror . . . until Rhys let out a "Pffttt" and began laughing his ass off. I followed suit, laughing at the ridiculous suggestion. Then, a few seconds later, I stopped laughing. *Oh my God, we were all high!* The fire we had been working all day must have been a cannabis field, and a good-sized one at that.

We told Blue and Steve, and they shook their heads in disbelief. None of us had any experience to tell us what being high felt like, so we all started looking around at one another, laughing and panicking at the same time.

"Oh crap," I murmured. "Steve's eyes are bloodshot!"

"Steve's eyes are always bloodshot," replied Blue. He was right, of course, and we enjoyed another good laugh. Everything was a lot funnier than usual that night.

We never did get that urine test, but I think we all knew what was going on. I was just glad to have finally experienced it, and I couldn't have picked a better group of guys to hit it with than good ol' Jolly 94.

Soon enough, thankfully, the wildfires died down, and it started to look like we'd get that much-anticipated break we were hoping for at the end of LOCCUST. But the summer of 2008 wasn't through with us yet. Hurricane Ike was just about to hit Houston, Texas, so our team was mobilized to head down there and help pluck folks who were too stubborn to evacuate off of their roofs. The government didn't want another Katrina on its hands, so we stood ready to launch.

There were a few crews who landed in driveways and boarded the scared, cold survivors, but for the most part, we just spent a good deal of time searching, flying around in the crappy weather to see if anyone waved at us. We even had a few of our PJs patrolling a street looking for anyone who needed help. Rumor has it that the PJs actually commandeered a fire truck whose keys were left in the ignition, but I wasn't there to see that. Knowing those guys, I certainly wouldn't have put it past them, though.

After that mission, we did get something of a break. There were missions and training here and there during the next few months, but the focus was mainly on spinup training to get us ready to head to Afghanistan in the spring. As the date of my next deployment neared, I thought about all we had been through that summer. I had grown close to Team Hawk and had spent hundreds of hours in and out of the aircraft with Rhys, Finn, Steve, and others. I had no idea who I'd be crewed with in Afghanistan, and I trusted everyone in my unit, but I was really hoping that Steve would be my FE. I knew that he was one of our best, and I couldn't think of anyone I'd rather have my back in combat. Whoever I ended up flying with, I had a good feeling that this deployment would be a very different experience from the last. I was right.

SEVEN

THE TRIP OVER TO Afghanistan in 2009 was similar to the first, but this time around I was a seasoned pilot, I was with friends, and I knew what I was getting myself into. The only person I had left to win over was Doug Sherry, but I didn't spend much time worrying about him. Some people would always make generalizations about others based on their gender or race; once I finally decided to accept that, I found a great deal of peace. I couldn't change people. I could only be the best version of myself and see if that made them change themselves.

On the way over to Kandahar, we ended up getting delayed at Ramstein Air Base in Germany, so we had a day or two to burn while waiting for transport. Some of us decided to head out to one of the local breweries for a tour. Luckily for us, we went through the beer-tasting part of the tour before having to sit through the video on the brewery's history, so we had a great time trying to translate the German narration. It would be the last beer we would have for months.

Once we got to Kandahar, we met up with the squadron we would be replacing. They briefed us on the current conditions and acclimatized us to the area. Although most of us had already been to Afghanistan, some things had inevitably changed in the year and a half since we had been away. There were new procedures for getting gas, new places to drop off patients, and new bases to forward deploy to.

Personally, I had a lot more on the line this time. When I deployed with New York, I was tangentially aware that what we were doing was dangerous. I'd congratulated myself on my "bravery" for not being afraid to die. You would think that, given my experience, I'd be even more comfortable. But on this deployment, I was actually scared.

This time around I was afraid, not for myself, but because I had grown so close to my brothers- and sisters-in-arms from California. The thought of losing one of them was terrifying. I looked around the room and saw my friends, but I also pictured all of their kids, brothers, sisters, parents, and spouses. I didn't want any of my friends to be in danger, but there was no way around it. As I sat through my first briefing and listened to the analysis of the threat situation, I thought back to the first time I had ever taken fire.

Back in my 2007 deployment, when I was still a very young Co-Pilot, I had just returned from my first rotation in TK, where we had lost that ███████ ODA sergeant to the gunshot wound to his arm that had penetrated his chest. I had been assigned to a new crew, so I was flying with one of my role models in New York named AJ Wineberger. AJ usually stood about six inches over everyone else in the room, but his unassuming, quiet demeanor made him less intimidating, and his approachability contributed to his admirable leadership ability.

We were flying a Dutch intelligence officer who had an injured ankle from a FOB back to Kandahar at night. I was looking through my night-vision goggles at the ridgeline that was about level with the aircraft, thinking that it was a good thing we were so low. The moon was bright enough that we would be silhouetted against the sky if anyone was looking for us. About then I heard a muffled boom and saw a flash of light outside AJ's door at about four o'clock that illuminated the entire inside of the cockpit for a split second.

"Hey! Is someone taking pictures?" AJ barked into the mic. "Keep your friggin' lights off!"

I kept quiet, wondering what in the hell had just happened. Then a steady stream of excited Dutch started pouring through my headset. After about thirty seconds of anxious charades between the Gunner and our patient, we realized he was telling us that it was an RPG—a rocket-propelled grenade—exploding outside the door. It was a little surreal, and while I felt a lot of adrenaline, I wasn't really scared. AJ quickly took evasive action, and we hightailed it back home.

Two years later, though, surrounded by my Rescue brothers and sisters, I knew the stakes were higher for me this time. I would do anything, fly into anything, to keep them safe. I looked over at Steve, and he nodded back at me. Maybe he was having the same thoughts.

As the meeting broke up, one of our senior pilots, Mat Wenthe, came over to chat with us. Mat came to us from active duty, where he was a rock-star pilot and a Weapons School graduate. The Weapons School is the Air Force's version of the Navy's famous Top Gun School. Mat was sharp, witty, and funny—definitely the cool kid that everyone wanted to fly with. He looked like sort of a shorter, better-looking Vince Vaughn with a high-and-tight haircut. Often paired with Doug Sherry on a crew, Mat had an uncanny ability to crack a joke that could put Doug in his place without alienating him or pissing him off. You couldn't help but like Mat—he was the perfect personality to balance out the much harsher Doug.

Mat had an important subject to discuss with us—choosing a call sign. It was standard for each incoming squadron to pick a new one. For example, the New York unit had been known as Yankee. So, you would hear "Yankee One Eight inbound for fuel" on the radios. We didn't have anything picked out yet, so we asked him for any suggestions. He suggested we use "Pedro," which I thought was odd. Why would we be Pedro? Because California bordered Mexico? Was it a play on the movie *Napoleon Dynamite*?

Later, I was embarrassed to learn that it was a name I should have known from Rescue history. It was a nod to the HH-43 rescue helicopters in Vietnam in the 1960s who used the call sign Pedro. The HH-43 pilots from Vietnam have an incredibly rich and brave history, not to mention a stellar reputation. It would be an honor to carry the Pedro call sign, and it would be an everyday reminder of the enormous responsibility we had to carry on the honorable Rescue tradition.

This would technically be my first time deployed with California, but it didn't feel like it. I could remember in 2007 when I was augmenting the 33rd Rescue Squadron out of Kadena Air Base, Japan, I had been thrilled to be tasked with a mission that would have us working side by side with the California unit. We had intel that Osama bin Laden had been spotted in northwest Pakistan, and they were planning a huge operation to try to take him out.

We had flown into Bagram Air Base in the capital city of Kabul to gear up and do some mission planning. It didn't matter that my unit was there doing medevac, and California was there supporting the CSAR mission. We were all CSAR assets, so we would all support this mission together.

We pre-positioned in the middle of nowhere near Jalalabad, Afghanistan, in the northeast part of the country, close to the border with Pakistan. Our crews would sit alert alongside the California unit, ready to go in if the sh*t hit the fan and the op went south. On the night our Special Forces teams were going to hit their target, I was standing outside our command tent, ruminating about the gravity of the event and hoping that we might be dealing a serious blow to Al-Qaeda. Sitting on the back of a four-wheeler, listening to some of the California guys inside the tent laugh and play pocket tanks, I caught some movement out of the corner of my eye.

I turned to look, but all I could see was two glowing green dots about the size of quarters floating toward me. I froze. It was one of our Special Forces team leaders, gliding over the rocks wearing his night-vision goggles. Behind him trailed more floating green globes as they marched single file through the night. They were utterly silent. It was both eerie and beautiful. They passed me without a sideways glance.

They were gone like wind across the desert, silent and powerful. I returned to the tent to monitor the intel reports, hoping with all my might that I would never see them again. If I did, it would mean that something had gone terribly wrong and I had to go out and rescue them.

We weren't called out that night, but we also didn't get bin Laden. The operation had afforded me the chance to hang out with my California buddies, and it made me feel like I was contributing to our military's presence in the theater. Rescue was immensely fulfilling, but it also felt good to be so close to such a monumental event. Even if we didn't succeed that night, I knew we would eventually.

——— • ———

During my first deployment two years earlier, we spent the majority of our time at KAF or forward deployed to TK. This time around, we would still be going back and forth between KAF and TK, but now we would be spending half our time at Camp Bastion. Bastion was in the heart of the Helmand River Valley, and our time there would present us with a much higher threat level than anything we experienced in 2007.

The Helmand River is one of the main irrigation sources for southern Afghanistan. In the 1950s and '60s, America spent more than eighty million dollars to help develop the area, using the Tennessee Valley Authority and the Hoover Dam as benchmarks. Today, the presence of the irrigation infrastructure makes the area the perfect place to grow poppies for heroin, so it is fiercely defended by the Taliban. As of 2015, almost a third of all casualties from the war in Afghanistan have occurred in the Helmand province.

After a few weeks in Kandahar, we started rotating different crews through Bastion. I was happy to be on the first rotation, ready to get back into the action I had missed so much. It's not that I enjoyed being shot at, but I preferred this type of flying to the more mundane, air-traffic-controlled flying back in the States. It's like the difference between being a race car driver and a bus driver. No matter how much you love to drive, you still have to find something that goes your speed.

Bastion was kind of like Tarin Kowt in that there wasn't a ton of administrative bullsh*t to deal with, and we didn't have many of the comforts of Kandahar either. But Bastion was better than TK in another way—this time, there were enough of us to be split into two shifts, twelve hours on and twelve hours off. We spent some of our downtime playing video games and relaxing, but the tempo was still so high at Bastion that there was a lot less time for relaxation. We spent most of our time doing mission planning or getting ready for our next mission, as well as trying to cram gray food in brown sauce down our throats while keeping an ear out for the medevac mission alarm to sound.

Settling into our accommodations at Bastion wasn't

difficult. They weren't much different from a lot of the places I had laid my head—dusty, bad food, tents, rocks, and long hours on shift. Bring it.

We slept in large tents, shared by a couple dozen people. Unfortunately, as a female, I wasn't allowed to be housed with my crew this time. Other than a few miscommunications when it came to catching rides in to work, it wasn't a big deal. On the flip side, though, the few times when I have been housed with men instead of just women, there have been absolutely no issues. After all, if teenage girls and boys can sleep together in a school gym during a lock-in, professional adult men and women should be able to share a giant tent with a few dozen of our fellow squadron members without us all making a bigger deal out of it than it has to be.

One afternoon, in June 2009, I was on shift, watching some of the PJs play Halo and waiting my turn, when I heard a 9-Line drop. I hopped up from my seat and looked over the shoulder of the intel troop to see if we were about to launch. It looked like the mission was a go, so I started heading out to the truck. At Kandahar and TK you could jog out to the aircraft, but at Bastion we were too far away from the flight-line. At the sound of "REDCON ONE" on the radios, you would see a caravan of old pickups and golf carts kicking up dust behind them as they rushed out to the birds.

Moments later, just as I was starting the truck, I heard "REDCON ONE" over the radio. We were a go. Our Danish comrades were pinned down near the river and needed us to pull out some of their wounded. I pulled up to the driveway and waited as my crew shouted "Yee-haw" and jumped in. After a quick head count to make sure no one was left behind, we pulled away into the dusty afternoon heat, ready to save a few lives.

When we arrived on the flightline, I jumped out of the truck and started jogging to the aircraft. I knew that this would piss off Doug, who was always telling us not to run. But adrenaline was high when we were headed out on a mission, so most of us at least jogged. One of the Flight Engineers was jogging next to me, and he started pulling ahead. So I picked up the pace. He grinned and looked sidelong at me and started sprinting. I kicked it into high gear and passed him, just as I heard Doug yell to us, "Slow is safe and safe is fast, douchers!"

Just as I felt on top of the world, I stepped on a patch of gravel on the cement pad next to the helicopter. In slow motion, my feet slipped out from under me and up over my head as my checklist exploded and a million pieces of paper flew everywhere.

My FE was right on my heels and almost stepped on me, but he thought fast and hurdled over me like an Olympic track star. He couldn't stop laughing, hand to his chest as he struggled to catch his breath, but he managed to ask me if I was okay.

"Sh*t!" I exclaimed as I scrambled to gather my checklist. I looked up and saw Doug walking to his aircraft, shaking his head. For some reason, every time I did something stupid, I would look up and see him watching.

Doug and Mat would be flying in flight lead in front of us, and I took a moment to wonder if they felt as secure on our wing as I did on theirs. Despite not being Doug's favorite person, I knew he'd take a bullet for me. I only hoped he knew I would do the same for him.

I composed myself and got back into character as we spun up to launch. It was business time, and we fell into the checklist rhythm that was so familiar to us. We knew that this was just like any other mission, but we also knew we were twice as likely to see a hot landing zone out here in Helmand. We flew out to the south with our sister ship, test-fired our guns, and headed into the poppy fields. It wasn't long before we made contact on the radio with someone with a Danish accent who directed us to the point-of-injury landing zone.

We looked below us and saw some one-story, mud-caked adobe houses about 150 feet from the north-south-running river parallel to it. Between the houses and the river, our allies popped green smoke, and we started our approach to the field as our sister ship circled above. We flew over the houses to land in a grassy area with the river around fifty feet off our nose. About ten feet from the ground, we heard four booms in succession, approximately one second apart. There was no way to know if it was friendly forces shooting outbound as opposed to the inbound impacts of enemy mortar rounds, but I crossed my fingers it was the good guys.

We landed and sent our PJs out to get the patients as fast as possible. I could hear the Danish soldiers talking excitedly on the radio, and although I couldn't understand them, I had a good idea what they were saying. We were under attack. They knew they had to protect us long enough to get their buddies out of there if their injured comrades were going to survive the day. I searched the sky, looking for our sister ship. When I spotted her, I was relieved to see muzzle flashes coming from the fifty-caliber machine guns, raining hate on whoever was trying to take us out.

In order to fire our weapons, a US aircraft has to have a positively identified enemy fire point of origin, eyes on their sister ship, eyes on all friendly forces in the area, and an understanding of what's behind their target (to prevent civilian casualties). If they were lighting someone up behind us, then those guys were doing something to deserve it.

We were eager to get in, pick up our guy, and get the hell out, but we waited for what seemed like ages and our patient still didn't appear. Our PJs showed up after about two minutes, fast-walking in with the stretcher. Once they were loaded up, I called up to Mat and Doug to tell them we were pulling pitch to take off. This is the phase of flight where we're most vulnerable, and our sister ship needs to be ready to cover our takeoff. There is an art form to timing this perfectly. Ideally, the aircraft on the ground calls a thirty-second warning to let the cover ship get set up to make a run, but sometimes those thirty seconds can turn into ten seconds. We couldn't wait any longer to pull out, so the cover ship had to bank around hard to lay enough lead to get the enemy to duck. If they do it right and you're lucky, the enemy doesn't even notice that you're taking off.

We picked up and headed for the river. I heard the fifty-cal of our sister ship laying down cover for us at about fourteen beautiful rounds per second. We banked left and headed north along the river before falling in behind our lead bird. Mat and Doug had just saved our asses, but we did this for each other all the time. We never thanked each other. We were just doing our jobs, sometimes four or five times a day.

Every mission was critical, each life precious. We would gladly lay down our lives for one another. Our mission statement, "These things we do that others may live," was emblazoned on our walls, patches, T-shirts, and hats. However, there was one mission during that deployment that none of us was happy about.

In June 2009, a 9-Line dropped on us for a Marine in the southern part of the Helmand River Valley at a FOB called Dwyer. To get to Dwyer, we would have to fly through some of the most dangerous parts of the valley. Our route would take us past Lashkar Gah and Marjah. But it wasn't the danger that bothered us. It was the injury.

Apparently this young Marine thought it would be a good idea to pleasure himself using the lubricant we used on our guns. The only problem with that was the compound we used to maintain our weapons wasn't just a lubricant. It was also a chemical cleaner used to break down rust, carbon, and other buildup, and while it may not hurt to get some of it on your hands, it's best to keep it away from your eyes, mouth, and, well, other sensitive areas.

It would almost have been funny, if it hadn't meant that two aircraft and fourteen people were risking their lives to evacuate this guy. There's no such thing as a safe mission.

Every time we launched, we flew over the wire and into possible enemy fire. Luckily, the mission was uneventful, and we returned our fallen comrade to the medical care he needed. I'm sure he got a great call sign out of it and learned a valuable lesson. Let's just hope there wasn't any permanent damage.

———— ● ————

In addition to our TOC, there was an operations command for the entire base, where we would go once a shift to get a briefing on the current condition of the American, Brit, and Danish missions going on in the area. It was a good chance to get to know the folks we were supporting and find out how they felt their medevacs were going. There were several different groups responsible for medevac. In addition to the regular Dustoff Army Black Hawks, there were British Chinooks and others. We would keep an ear out for mention of Pedro to ensure we were supporting them to the best of our ability. This meeting was also where we could bring concerns about operations from our end, or issues we were having on the base.

One day, the British sergeant major approached our first sergeant, Red, to talk to him about how cramped the US quarters were. He was part of the British 2nd Rifles Battle Group, a unit that had had a particularly rough summer and had lost a lot of good soldiers.

"Red, can I have a quick second? I know you lot are sleeping on top of each other in that tent of yours. As you know, we've got space, and, well . . . The lads took a vote, and we'd like you boys to come stay with us."

Pedro 15 and 16.

Red wasn't sure what to say to that. He knew it was an emotional decision for them to make, as it was almost a way of admitting that their comrades weren't coming back. He couldn't believe that they'd had so many casualties.

"Thank you. Thank you so much. We'd be honored to," Red responded somberly.

With a serious nod, the sergeant major went back to work. Our willingness to fly into anything to pull out the wounded had gained the Pedros a reputation that garnered the respect and admiration of the ground forces we were supporting. That sort of relationship was the best compliment you could give to a rescue squadron.

The Danes were another group we grew close to. One of the missions that Mat Wenthe flew under the Pedro name ended up in the Danish documentary movie *Armadillo* and resulted in one of the more well-known radio exchanges of the whole deployment. The Danish Special Forces unit we were supporting had been kicking ass for about ten months until the summer of 2009. In June of that year, they were in the middle of one hell of a firefight and were taking some heavy casualties. Seeing their brothers take so many injuries had the unit pretty shaken up, but inspiration soon came from above.

Mat and Doug, along with their sister ship carrying a crew from Kadena, Japan, went in guns a-blazing and pulled out their wounded. Knowing that they weren't in this battle alone reinvigorated the Danes to such an extent that it turned the tide of the battle and helped them overcome the insurgents they were fighting. On their way out, a Danish commander grabbed a ground controller's radio and keyed the mic with a message.

"Pedros, you have given my Vikings brave inspirations today. Thank you."

It was just about the coolest thing we had ever heard.

A few days later, one of the men who had been in that battle sent us a poem he had written about that portion of the fight. It translates as:

The angels who came from above
Even when the smoke from their rifles had not yet stopped
They took our wounded Viking and brought him to Valhalla.
Now stand by our side again, you angel, we owe everything.

We were so touched by this that our unofficial squadron motto became *"Fortis Incito,"* which is Latin for "incite bravery."

From then on out, we were determined to fly all of our missions in such a way that we could give the ground forces "brave inspirations."

After a few weeks at Bastion, it was time for our crew to rotate back to KAF for somewhat of a break. We would still be flying medevac missions, and we'd still be getting shot at, but we'd be pulling two or three flights per shift as opposed to the four or five per shift at Bastion. Better yet, the enemy presence was much more scattered and less organized in Kandahar. I was looking forward to the break, but I would miss Bastion. I couldn't help wanting to be in the middle of the action. I was addicted to the adrenaline of it. Every time I left, I felt like I was abandoning the incredible people we were supporting out there. But it was time. We had to load up the birds and head back to KAF.

———— • ————

We settled back in at KAF and began sitting alert the next day. At shift change, I went out to the aircraft to run it up and check the radios, just like I had always done. Some sixth sense that gave me a good radar for bullsh*t made me look up and over my right shoulder. I could see some high-ranking brass heading my way, but I couldn't make out who it was. He looked vaguely familiar, but I couldn't really see him through the crowd of sycophants surrounding him. I went about my business, spinning up the navigation system and flipping through the radios. A few minutes later, when I looked up again, I could see the brass and his entourage were making a beeline for me. Great. I shut everything down and started climbing out of the bird.

"Lieutenant Jennings."

I knew that old familiar bark anywhere. I had been a captain for years; there was only one person who would still call me by my old outdated rank. The man towered over the rest of the group; I swear I could almost see the disdain he held for me dripping off of him. It was Major Johnson, my first commander from Japan, the one whose first conversation with me consisted of a discussion of my time of the month, and the guy who'd let me stand in his office holding my salute as he refused to salute me back.

He was now a full-bird colonel. Not many officers attained the prestigious rank, but it didn't surprise me he was one of them. He always did have a penchant for taking credit for the good stuff other people were responsible for, and for stepping on the people who got in his way. I was a little surprised he hadn't been prosecuted for discrimination by now, but I guess he still didn't work with that many women.

"Hi," I replied casually.

I refused to call him "sir." I doubted very seriously he could make any trouble for me with my current chain of command. We didn't take rank as seriously in the Guard; it was more about competence and credibility. Colonel Johnson had apparently recently taken over as the Maintenance Group Commander at Kandahar. I was so happy that we were on a rotation that would enable me to escape back to Bastion again soon and away from the likes of him.

"'Hi'? Is that all you have for me?" He turned back to his entourage. "Lieutenant Jennings always wanted to be a pilot, but you guys know how unlikely it is to get picked up off of active duty for a slot. I always knew she could do it, but I had to be really hard on her to toughen her up first." He looked back at me with a creepy smile that I had never seen before. "She owes it all to me."

"Yeah. Good to see you. Gotta run . . . On alert . . ." I walked past him with my gear back toward the TOC. It was a long walk, but I didn't hear or see him on the way back. I haven't seen him since, but I'm sure he still thinks I have a lot to thank him for—and he was right. Colonel Johnson definitely gave me a lot of motivation to go to pilot training and prove to *myself* that he had been wrong about me.

Throughout my life I had known tragedy and triumph. Love and loss. Strength and weakness. I had come a long way from that scared little girl sitting on the fireplace, watching in terror as my sister got her ass beat. Everything I had experienced and all of the leaders—bad and good—from whom I had learned would soon culminate in the biggest challenge I would ever face. I would be tested to the extreme. Every pilot I knew wondered exactly how they would handle the ultimate trial. In hindsight I guess I should consider myself lucky—I was about to find out.

EIGHT

IN JULY 2009, ABOUT halfway through my five-month deployment, I heard a familiar voice as I walked into the morning brief. I'd know that mellow Caribbean accent anywhere. When I turned the corner, I saw the broad shoulders and big smile of TieJie "TJ" Jones, my buddy from California. Our commander, Lieutenant Colonel Rhys Hunt, started to address the group, welcoming our comrades who had just arrived. TJ stood next to Colonel Hunt, wearing his signature troublemaker's smirk. On the colonel's other side was a new guy I'd never met before. He was only an inch or two taller than me, a little older, and had an air of serenity around him that seemed to balance out the restless energy in the room.

Midway through any deployment, some of us would go home, and a few of us who had been left behind would come in to replace them. I was losing my Gunner and my Aircraft Commander, and I was eager to hear who my new crew would be. I was of course hoping that Steve and I would stay together, though it wasn't a given. They could and often did change up crews at the drop of a hat, but I didn't particularly want to fly with anyone except Steve. Anything we did together took half as long. After our time running drug missions in California that previous summer, we could almost read each other's minds through the call-and-response dance of Co-Pilots and Flight Engineers.

Colonel Hunt looked over at me. "MJ and Steve, Teej is your new Gunner." YES! This was going to be great—TJ was a top-notch Gunner. Now, who would be sitting in the seat next to me?

"I want you all to welcome to our squadron Major George Dona. He's coming to us from active duty, and this is his first time in country. MJ, take good care of him."

The new guy. I looked my new Aircraft Commander over and gave him a nod. For his first time in Afghanistan, he didn't look very worried. George smiled, showing sun-worn wrinkles around his eyes. Even standing ramrod straight, hair high and tight in the same short cut all of the guys wore, his vibe still screamed Hawaiian surfer dude. George Dona. We'd heard about him. None of us had ever flown with him before, but his reputation from active duty was stellar. When not required to be in a flight suit, George was known to immediately change into his natural uniform of flip-flops and board shorts. He and TJ were going to fit right into our Kandahar gazebo team, I thought.

When the brief ended, we gathered around the recent arrivals.

"Teej!" I said, and he grabbed my hand and pulled me in to bump shoulders—even though his shoulder hit the top of my head.

"Welcome aboard, George—the men you'll fly with here are top-notch," I heard Doug Sherry say, around the unlit cigar in his mouth. It was seven A.M.—seriously, did he sleep with that thing in his mouth? George wore a smile at all times, so I couldn't tell if he'd caught the *men* comment. I was pretty sure Sherry didn't mean it as a pointed jab in my direction, but it just solidified for me once again how utterly invisible I was to him. He never missed an opportunity to show me—intentionally or not—that he didn't think of me as a part of his team.

Later that day, we walked out to our Pave Hawk with the new team for a dry run, George caught in the crossfire of our banter.

"You haven't flown with MJ before," Steve informed him jokingly. "Please don't judge all of Team Hawk by our one weak link." On cue, he deftly stepped out of the way before I could slug him. Experience had taught him well.

TJ waved a dismissive hand. "You sure about that, Steve? I hear that it's the Flight Engineer who is the weak link on Hawk."

"Shut up and go oil your barrel, Gunner," Steve shot back, laughing.

George smiled and nodded, not saying much. Clearly he took the quiet approach. I could tell he was waiting to see if all this cockiness bore out when we got in the air. And it did.

As soon as we got the bird up in the air and crossed the fence out of Kandahar, we all sat a little straighter and looked around a little more intently. Within a few days, it felt like the best crew I'd ever flown with. Steve, TJ, George, and me. We had our rhythms coordinated, and we quickly trusted each other's instincts. It felt like a true team.

It was a damn good thing the team managed to gel so quickly. Only two weeks after George arrived, I would experience the longest day of my life with them.

———— ⬥ ————

In the early afternoon of July 29, 2009, I was sitting in the left-side pilot's seat of our Pave Hawk, Pedro 15 (or "Pedro one five"). My crew had just come on shift, so I was checking the radios and had the main power spun up. Rows of other helos sat waiting on the bone-dry taxiway, heat shimmering off it in waves. Even in my flight suit, the temperature didn't get to me anymore, but I tied the arms around my waist to help me cool off. The heat could fatigue a crew pretty quickly, but it could wreak more havoc with the aircraft, decreasing the power of our engines and slowing us down. In this kind of climate, we flew with both pilots' doors off, in order to ventilate the cabin and help us to see the ground when the dust clouds engulfed the helicopters.

I reached down to align the navigation system with the GPS satellites. When I looked back up, I saw George and the team jogging toward me across the hot tarmac.

When George reached the aircraft, he flung a piece of

MJ in the co-pilot seat.

paper across the seat to me. I slapped it down on the console with my gloved hand before the wind snatched it. As George hauled himself up into the chest-high cockpit and strapped himself in, I scrutinized the paper, plugging in the coordinates off it. By the time Steve and TJ jumped in the back and put on their helmets, we were just about ready to fly.

"Battery on, APU on," Steve read over the intercom, going through the scramble checklist.

I had already spun those up, so we were ahead of the game.

"Fuel selectors on, number-one engine, number-two engine."

My fingers found the switches before Steve finished reading them off.

Behind me, I heard TJ pop open an ammunition box, feeding the belt into his door gun, and slapping the cover down with a clap. He and Steve hooked into a lanyard so they could move around the cabin and—if they had to survey the landscape below—safely hang out the doors while we flew. Instinctively, I reached a hand back and touched my rifle, making sure it was right where it belonged, behind my seat.

The mission sheet said we were on our way to rescue three critical American soldiers. Their convoy had hit an IED-complex ambush about twenty-five minutes out from Kandahar—well inside that "golden hour" when our medics could save almost anyone.

Our helo was nearly ready to go, and just in time, three PJs climbed on board. Short and muscle-bound, they looked like G.I. Joe action figures, with all the high-speed gear laced into the webbing of their body armor and short GUA-5 assault rifles pinned to their chests. The PJs are the most unsung heroes of the war. Few people back home have heard of Air Force Special Ops, but every grunt on the ground has. Besides making the medical decisions, the PJs take charge in the unlikely event that we end up in ground combat.

Today I recognized one of the three—Technical Sergeant ███████████—a rock-solid airman I'd flown with before. He was the PJ team lead, and his team was ready to go. The soldiers we were going to rescue didn't even know how lucky they were that he was on board.

Once the PJs were strapped in, we were off. We cleared our takeoff with the radio tower and flew out across the fence in a gale of dust. We flew over Kandahar's civilian airport, where, despite the war going on all around them, you could see Afghans stepping down airplane gangways, wearing suits or robes or light-blue burkas. Once we had passed over the one straight, paved highway, all we could see ahead were imposing rocky hills.

After we flew north over the hills, the landscape started to turn green—a seemingly pretty change from the dusty dry brown that surrounds the base and most of central Kandahar. But after three tours, I'd learned the downside of a fertile landscape. In Helmand at Bastion, it would have been poppy fields, but here in Kandahar, they were more likely to be pomegranate orchards and lush grapevines trailing over tall mudbrick walls. It looked idyllic, sure, until a man in cheap shades and a turban pops out of the scenery with a rocket-propelled grenade to shoot down your helicopter.

I saw a cluster of farmhouses ahead—another thing I'd learned to avoid.

"Come right thirty," I said.

George acknowledged with a sharp bank of the aircraft, changing our heading to thirty degrees right of our course. He had more years as a pilot than me, but no ego to prevent him from responding to my input. He and I had gotten along well from the start, and I knew what an enormous responsibility I had to him as the combat-seasoned veteran on board. He would be depending on me to help him make decisions, and I wasn't planning to let him down.

Behind us our sister ship, Pedro 16, followed a course

skewed off to one side and behind us, both of us flying low and fast. Like us, Pedro 16 carried a handful of PJs and a crew of four. If one helo went down, the other should be able to rescue the entire second crew and the patients in need. Pedro 15 was lead ship this time—so Pedro 16 was our backup and would hang back and cover us with their door guns while we got the wounded out.

"Threat suppressed for now, over."

The radio traffic from two Army choppers supporting the hobbled convoy from the air was reporting that the firefight we were heading into was over, at least for the moment. The Army choppers were OH-58 Kiowa Warriors—nimble two-pilot helicopters with a giant bug's eye of a surveillance camera sitting on top of the rotors. They packed a punch, too—rocket launchers above one skid and a large-caliber machine gun over the other. It sounded like the Kiowas had pushed back the Taliban enough that we could make it in to grab the wounded without taking too much fire.

I got on the radio to Shamus 34, the Kiowa.

"Shamus three four, Pedro copies."

There was a silence. Our sister ship broke through the static: "Pedro fifteen, did you catch that? Shamus three four reported they have suppressed the threat to the convoy for now, but there may still be enemy forces to the south."

Of course we'd caught it. That's why I'd responded to the Kiowa! I was confused, but very quickly it dawned on us: no one had heard our reply.

George looked at me and rolled his eyes. Our own radio

jammers, put in place to scramble the enemy's communication efforts, sometimes left our aircraft deaf and mute. It was possible we had a malfunction, but we had tested the radios before we left. Regardless, now we'd have to relay all our communication through our sister ship. And when you're flying into hot enemy territory, it's not really the best time to play "telephone."

A high-pitched voice came across the FM receiver. "I . . . pickup . . . out of here . . . wounded . . . now . . ." Even with the broken-up transmission, we could all hear that the soldier was scared.

"Fox-Mike bent," I said to my crew, meaning the FM radio wouldn't be reliable today.

"Yeah, comms are sh*t." George nodded, saying aloud what I'd been thinking.

Before I could worry much about the radios, our helo cleared a ridge, and the broken-down convoy appeared in the valley below us, like gladiators in a Roman arena. From our vantage point on high, the line of drab US Army trucks looked like a toy train, blocked in by a scorched crater. Taliban gunmen who were hiding in the village to the south had the whole squad pinned down.

"Contact," George said. "I have them three o'clock low."

"Roger, contact," Steve confirmed.

"Pedro one six. One five in the blind. We're coming right two seven zero landing north of the convoy," reported George, telling our sister ship we would be doing a right turn all the way around to face west.

George didn't even know if our sister ship could hear him, but going "in the blind" meant that he would continue to transmit just in case Pedro 16 could hear us. He was going to swing around in a horseshoe pattern and land to the right of the convoy, putting the reported enemy activity to the south, out our left door. That way the armored trucks between us and the enemy guns would provide cover for the PJs and the wounded while we loaded up the helo. We'd drop in to allow two of the three PJs to jump off. Then we'd pull pitch, heading back above the ridgeline, allowing the PJs to work on the wounded without having to scream over our rotor wash. When they were ready, they'd call the third PJ, still on board our aircraft, on their inter-team radio to bring us back.

It was a good plan. George's confidence, when he was only a few weeks in this hostile country, continued to impress me.

Then he did something spectacular.

A normal helo approach is a forty-five-degree-angle glide into the landing zone, slowly bleeding off airspeed on the way down. Normal means predictable, though, and with Taliban guns ready to take target practice on us, predictable just means an easy way to die. Instead, George flew full-speed at the last truck in the convoy. It felt almost like an autorotation. I'll admit I was holding my breath the entire time. I had full faith in him, but given the fact that we had just started flying together, I hovered my hands over the controls, ready to take over if he was going to plant us into the ground.

"George?" I said, just about at my limit for comfort.

"I got it . . . ," he said, reading my mind. And he did have everything under control. Just forty feet before impact, he suddenly pulled the nose up, bleeding off the airspeed in an instant, flying alongside the convoy, rotors pitched back like a falcon pumping its wings to land in a treetop. I'd never seen anything like it. You can feel in your body when a helo is out of control, and George never came anywhere close to that. He wasn't macho hotdogging, like I'd seen with Top Gun wannabes in flight school; George knew the limits of the aircraft and pushed against them to do what needed to be done. He flew like I tried to—using the aircraft as an extension of his body rather than a vehicle in which to sit.

The PJs jumped out and ran toward the convoy, one after another. Tech Sergeant ███████████, the PJ I'd flown with before, was still on board. And thank goodness he was, because that was about when the day started to go very, very wrong.

I heard a crack like a baseball bat hitting a home run, and then the helo's windshield shattered right in front of my eyes. Through the web of splintered glass, the Kandahar desert hills stretched out for miles in front of me. But all I saw was the perfectly round little hole in the middle of the windshield, where the hot desert air was whistling in from outside.

My right arm felt warm and wet, but I ignored it. I was thinking only about the wrecked windshield. It was brand-new—our maintainers had just spent hours in the searing heat replacing it the day before. I'd joked with the crew chiefs that we should just kick the old glass out instead of going by the book and painstakingly removing it in one piece. All their work was ruined now.

Maybe they'll kick this one out?

One look at George's horrified face reeled me back to the present tense. His lips moved, and I knew the whole crew was shouting at me over the intercom, but for an instant all I could hear was the high whine of the engine and the deep, comforting thunder of the rotor blades. I followed George's gaze to the blood spreading over my exposed arm and the leg of my flight suit. I had the strangest split-second moment of relief that I had tied my sleeves around my waist in an attempt not to overheat. Now I wouldn't have to patch a bullet hole in the arm of my uniform.

How can I be hit in two places if there's only one hole in the windscreen?

Snap out of it, I told myself. I quickly assessed my situation.

"I'm hit, but . . . I can still fly," I told them, fully confident that I was telling the truth. "I'm hit, but I'm okay!"

"Are you really okay?" There were four voices shouting all at once in my headset.

George pulled the helo up in the air and out of rifle range as ████, the PJ team lead, squeezed over the console to look at my injuries. With his bulk and all his medical gear, he barely fit, and it probably didn't help that I was trying to swat him away so I could get back to the mission at hand.

Shrapnel peppered my right forearm and right thigh. The arm wounds were superficial. I couldn't see the leg wound, but the spreading bloodstain was worrying—first it was the size of a grapefruit, and then it grew larger and larger until it was the size of a basketball. But after a few minutes the stain stopped spreading, and I began to breathe easier. I'd never been shot before, but I'd flown so many wounded troops that I could tell a serious wound from a paper cut. No reason to call off the mission.

In the back, TJ was doing just that. "I repeat . . . Pedro one five Co-Pilot hit . . . We're RTB . . ."

Return to base!

I didn't blame him—I was covered in blood, but I was in no way ready to head back to base.

"Gunner—hold that," I said. I could sense the look he was giving me without even having to turn around. They were all looking at me in disbelief. Even George had started to look a little pale through his dark Hawaiian complexion.

"Look, guys, I swear!" I reached my arm up over my head and moved it side to side. "I have full range of motion, and my leg has already stopped bleeding. We've got three cat-A soldiers down there. Let's get back to it."

After all, we had to give them "brave inspirations," right? Category A meant urgent, and I wasn't going to be the reason they bled out. I had lost enough soldiers to this war already, and I knew that if we lost them I would never forgive myself for heading back to KAF.

Steve was the only one who didn't seem to object. After so much time together flying on drug-eradication missions in California, he knew me well enough: if I said I was good, I was good. He knew I would never endanger my own crew out of some sense of bravado.

After a moment of silence, George piped up to the guys in back.

"You guys okay with going back in?"

He got affirmative answers from everyone, so he began to turn the aircraft back toward the convoy. Steve broke in that if we were going back in, we should enable the contingency power switch, a switch that would give us extra power if we needed it but is used only in dire circumstances as it can burn up your engines if you're not careful. I flipped it on, and we headed back toward the convoy.

Right on time, a familiar voice broke in over the radio: "Pedro one five, Guardian's ready for pickup." It was one of our PJs from the ground. They had no idea we'd been hit.

Unbeknownst to us, the PJs had gotten separated at the convoy and were not in communication with each other. The jammers had affected their inter-team radio, and only one of the PJs had made contact with the patients. He called us to land, hoping that the second PJ would see us touch down and run out to jump on board.

"Copy. Tell them we're inbound," George told the PJ team lead.

Then the headset crackled: "Pedro one five, one six . . . bent gun."

Bent gun. Sh*t, they were having a weapons malfunction. Our sister ship was telling us they had a broken gun and would be able to support us out of only one side of their bird. The only thing worse than returning to the scene where you got shot is doing it when your support ship can't fire one of its guns to defend you. *What else could possibly go wrong?*

"Roger. Grinder." George, cool as a cucumber, was calling for the two ships to switch roles.

Protocol states that if your support ship is impaired, you become the support ship. We would cover Pedro 16 with our two working guns as they landed to pick up the PJs and the wounded.

"Negative. We don't have the power," came the reply from command in Pedro 16, fast and a little frantic. "We're too heavy. We can't do it."

George and I exchanged a silent glance. I guess our radios were working again, because the other AC had clearly understood that we needed them to go in next but was refusing.

It was true that it was a lot of extra weight to ask Pedro 16 to lift, with three patients on the ground, our two PJs, plus their own full crew on board, but there are always fixes to unforeseen problems. Instinctively, I ran through all the ways to do it. The easiest solution was for them to dump some fuel, then reroute after the pickup to a nearby refueling point. It could be done—but not without steady resolve by Pedro 16's pilot.

He's lost his nerve, I thought to myself. George nodded like he could read my mind. He kept quiet, too. We didn't want to alarm the rest of our crew, but our silence didn't fool anyone. They'd all heard the pilot's voice. All of us who had done tours in Afghanistan had seen someone lose their courage. There was no coming back from that.

"Are you sh*tting me?" someone half shouted from the back of the bird. Now we'd have to stay lead, with Pedro 16 staying above, covering us with just one gun. At least the Kiowa Warriors had hung around and were still buzzing over the convoy. Their pods were about half full of rockets, which would give us some extra cover.

George quickly yanked and banked, about to execute the same heart-stopping dive-landing next to the convoy he had pulled off moments before, but he was now faced with a difficult choice. He could land to the same spot and be predictable to the enemy, or he could land somewhere else that hadn't been cleared and risk landing on a mine or other improvised explosive device (IED). The convoy we were evac'ing the patient from had been disabled after they'd hit their own IED, so we knew there were likely more. George decided the lesser of two evils was to land on the same spot. However, while the small bullet that had splintered into my arm and thigh had been a dumb-luck shot from a rifle, we were about to find out that one of the enemy's heavy belt-fed machine guns had since been trained on our landing zone.

As the wheels touched down, heavy slugs from their machine gun began to hit us hard, beating out a steady rhythm into our aircraft. I could feel more than hear the big rounds slamming into us. They shook my insides. As rounds impacted the tail and slowly started moving forward as the enemy maneuvered the heavy gun, our eight-ton aircraft rocked like a little rowboat on the ocean. The row of armored trucks gave us little protection from the barrage. The enemy was firing from the high ground at eleven o'clock.

The PJ who was off comm must have seen the hail of fire we were under and thought, *F that . . . I'm not gonna get shot trying to run to an aircraft that isn't taking off.* While one of the PJs and patients came out to the bird, a second PJ stayed with the convoy. With our hands full responding to failing systems and boarding patients, no one on board stopped to ask where he was.

When the tail malfunctions, a warning horn can be heard over the intercom. Since our tail was being shot to sh*t, the horn was drowning out anything we were trying to say to one another. It was all happening so fast that none of us thought to silence the horn with our cutoff switch, but we were on the ground for what had to be less than fifteen seconds.

With the sirens blaring over our intercom, we couldn't talk to one another in these crucial few seconds. However, from my vantage point closest to the convoy on the left side of the aircraft, I could see over my left shoulder that the patients were still being loaded. We couldn't lift during transfer because we'd hurt or kill someone. So I gave George the signal with my hand to hold and stay down on the ground, until I saw that the patients were safely on board.

This was an incredible show of steely nerves on George's part, let alone faith in the judgment of his Co-Pilot. He had very little prior knowledge of me other than the fact that he knew I was experienced and that I had gone through the same training he had. A lesser pilot would have panicked at the aircraft being rocked by heavy fire and might have just bolted, causing injury or death to the patients and soldiers loading them onto our aircraft.

Our sister ship and the two Kiowas couldn't help us. It was clear that the enemy had been planning this attack in the hopes of taking down a rescue helicopter. Insurgents were dug into the high ground with weapons aimed at the landing site. They had concealed their position to the extent that our cover ships could not determine a point of origin for the fire we were taking. We couldn't fire back; nor could our support ships. We were on our own.

TJ couldn't spot the enemy machine gun either, and he could hardly open fire while our patients were being loaded in. Not to mention, his gun was designed to fire down, not up. So he and his fifty-cal had to sit and wait, just taking the fire as the wounded soldiers were loaded into the left bay door.

Once I saw we were clear, I gave George the thumbs-up. With two pilots, one is always "outside" and the other "inside" the aircraft. George would watch the terrain and fly us back to the hospital at Kandahar Airfield. My job was to concentrate on the systems.

Many times, in a crisis, crews will make things worse by flipping the wrong switch in their haste. Pilots have been known to accidentally shut down a good engine while the other is on fire. As per our protocol, I was calling back to Steve to confirm all of the switches I was flipping, isolating hydraulics and such. While he was verbally confirming all of my actions, he actually had his hands full with manning his gun and trying to keep bad guys away long enough for us to get out of the landing zone (LZ). He wasn't even watching me. Given our history, he trusted me completely to be doing the right thing and thought he would serve us better searching for a point of origin for the incoming fire.

We barely had enough power to clear the terrain ahead of us, but thanks to Steve, we had engaged our contingency power switch on the way in. He had known when we went back in that we'd be facing a firefight. That decision, at this second, was saving our lives. If he had not thought of that on our way in, we would be a scorch mark on the desert floor today.

In our line of work, there is simply no worse feeling in the world than leaving a PJ or patient behind. The first thing we would normally do in this situation is turn around and go back in to get our missing PJ. However, things were about to go from bad to worse for us, and the aircraft we were flying would only be making one more landing in its lifetime.

George kept us flying low and fast, so the enemy would have a harder time drawing a bead on us against the sky—more brilliant flying on his part. Seconds after takeoff, though—and just as ▮▮▮▮ was realizing that for some reason, our third PJ wasn't on board—Steve said something that turned my blood cold.

"We've got fuel back here . . ." From the smell, I knew he meant that it was spewing into the cabin. I immediately looked at the fuel gauge to see how fast it was leaking. The number-one fuel tank on the left side of the aircraft wasn't just leaking—it was already empty—and the number-two tank wasn't far behind.

The two gas tanks are heavily armored, so the Taliban's machine gun rounds must have hit the tiny fuel line—for the second time today, a one-in-a-million shot. Each tank fed one of the Pave Hawk's jet engines, so now one of our engines was running on fumes. With this load on board, one engine wouldn't be able to keep us aloft. In an instant, I followed through a quick chain of logical events in my head. At the end of the chain, there was only one conclusion: us flaming out and hitting the ground burning. Any second now.

I instinctively threw the fuel selector into cross-feed, buying us a few minutes as the left engine started receiving fuel from the right tank. The bird kept flying. We hadn't planted into the terrain. Yet. *Thank God.* Here we are, about to crash on the desert floor, and instead of my life flashing before my eyes, I found myself imagining a crew recovering the wreckage. They'd load it all up into a Chinook and drag it back to Kandahar, and then the head of the investigation would say, "Hey, look—at least the Co-Pilot switched the number-one fuel selector into cross-feed."

Before I could breathe a sigh of relief, I looked at the fuel gauge. The needle for the right tank, now feeding both engines, was moving toward empty far too quickly.

There was only one option left.

"We need to land."

"Yeah, we're RTB," George replied. It came as no surprise that he was so focused on flying and on the surrounding terrain, he was unaware that our problem was bigger than a little fuel smell in the cabin. He didn't know about the empty tanks. We were RTB—returning to base, obviously. As in, *umm, yeah, what the hell else would we be doing?*

"We're not going to make it back to Kandahar," I stated, as clearly and calmly as I could. "We're pissing gas."

I saw the tiniest flicker of alarm on George's face.

"We have to either land over there"—I pointed to a flat spot of rocky sand just over to our right—"or we're going to crash . . . over there."

I pointed to a different ridge five miles off.

George didn't question a word I said. Without pause, he immediately pointed out a rocky spot where he planned to drop the helo. *There?* It was the right call. Harder to put land mines under rocks than sand. Our ordeal was far from over, and we weren't going home just yet. George needed zero distractions so he could concentrate on flying and landing our failing aircraft at the site, so an eerie hush came over us as he dove toward the rocky terrain.

Everyone did their part to prepare, but very soon there was nothing left to do except hold on tight for the crash. I reached my left arm up to the top of the doorway, placed my bleeding right hand on the console, and took a deep breath.

The bird was without hydraulic assistance to the controls as George guided us down—I could feel the strain through my seat, like driving an 18-wheeler with no power steering. As we touched down, far faster than usual, we could hear the bird crunch on impact. I felt a jarring crack in my mid-back, but the pain wouldn't slow me down, certainly not today. We had landed—a hard landing rather than a crash, thanks to George—all of us no worse for it. We were alive. George was an amazing pilot, and now his job was done. It was time for the PJs to take over.

The only thing to worry about now was the Taliban—and somehow figuring out how to get the hell out of there.

My hands moved quickly around the console, pulling levers and flipping switches, executing exactly as we'd been trained. I cut off the throttles and closed off the remaining fuel. The crew did the same, calmly and quickly running through the shutdown procedures we'd done hundreds of times.

Alongside that checklist, I tried to quiet my brain from playing out a script that I knew was no horror movie. It was our new reality: IEDs on the ground everywhere, no perimeter security, hills around us full of Taliban. I knew I'd fight to the death—far better that than being captured and marched through enemy territory with a bag over my head.

I reached around for my rifle, grabbed it, and slid out of the helo down to the rock-strewn terrain. After three tours in Afghanistan flying into countless combat zones, this was the first time I'd ever stepped outside the wire of an air base, on the ground in enemy territory.

With my back flat against the bird, I shuffled aft and

looked in the cabin, finally getting a good look at the patients we'd rescued. An older-looking soldier with his arm in a sling wore a vacant expression as if he'd already checked out. Not so the guy on the stretcher next to him—he looked plain pissed off. Straps on his chest and legs held him immobile. He was likely a spinal injury, but his arm could move, so he calmly made a request.

"Give me a f**king gun."

TJ handed the wounded soldier his sidearm and, despite the situation, we shared a smile. One more warrior on our side.

The third patient was another story. She looked young. I couldn't tell the extent of her injuries, just that panic had her shivering, despite the overwhelming Afghan summer heat. As she sat still on her seat, her eyes darted wildly around the cabin and outside to the hills. I bent close.

"Hey . . . hey, look at me." I locked on to her gaze.

"A rescue bird was just shot down in Afghanistan. Every aircraft in a one-hundred-mile radius just launched to come get us"—I got straight to the point—"so calm down. We'll be out of here soon."

As I stood up and turned back to TJ, I rolled my eyes.

He nodded in agreement. "Man, that's why they shouldn't let women on those convoys," he said to me quietly.

Covered in my own blood and soaked with jet fuel, I stared him down hard for a tick, but he didn't catch on.

"Are you f**king kidding me?"

TJ looked bewildered for a second; then it clicked.

"Oh, not you, MJ! You kick ass . . . ," he stammered.

I turned back to the bay door. I had no time to think about what it meant that TJ, who knew I was a warrior who would hold my own, somehow thought I was the exception. He still couldn't accept the fact that some women were every bit as capable as a guy in uniform.

After all, the pilot in Pedro 16 was a guy, and his loss of nerve was still fresh in my mind. Speaking of which, where the hell were they? Why weren't they landing next to us to get us out of Dodge? Not to mention, I was the one with blood all over my rifle arm, still ready to fight. Battle readiness had nothing to do with gender and everything to do with individual capability.

I shook it off and stepped in front of the open bay door. None of the patients had body armor, but I did, so I put myself between them and the hills. ███ stepped down next to me. He scanned the ridge off the tail of the helo, covering six to nine o'clock; I had nine to twelve o'clock off the nose. Standing shoulder to shoulder with a special-ops warrior like ███ felt good. This was what I was made for. I felt it in my gut. In the last hour, I'd been shot by the Taliban, had my aircraft riddled with bullets, and landed hard in enemy territory. *I can do this. I'm not scared.* At that moment, I wouldn't have switched spots with anyone in the world, because I knew I was the best person for the job.

It was a dangerous place to be, though—circled around a fuel-soaked, flightless bird, as TJ transmitted our location over an emergency radio channel.

"Mayday. Mayday . . . Pedro one five needs exfiltration."

Our sister ship, with the bent gun, stayed high overhead, showing no signs of being willing to land.

"Mayday. Mayday . . . Pedro one five needs exfil," he said again. I thought about the fact that the whole point of traveling in twos is so that one ship can rescue the other in an emergency situation. Pedro 16 had already declined to get our patients due to fears about weight; now we were asking them to lift even more. It didn't surprise me they were refusing to come down.

Still, TJ kept shouting into the radio, as explicitly as possible.

"MAYDAY! Pedro one six, f**king land and pick us up!"

Then the shooting started in earnest.

———— ◈ ————

I read intel reports later that had about 150 Taliban in the area. They had a clear plan: disable a convoy, injure a soldier, attract a medevac bird, and shoot it down. They never should have been able to pull it off, but there we sat, with more enemy fighters training their sights on us every minute. I was pretty sure that the significant enemy forces we had faced at the convoy minutes earlier were busy packing up their gear and heading our way to finish the job and kill or capture every last one of us. On the left side of the bird, bullets pinged off the rocks at our feet.

"Let's button up this side. We're taking too much fire." ▮▮▮▮ pointed with his head toward the other side. "Safer to go through the cabin," he added with a smile. "No need to get shot again."

I smiled back and threw my leg up into the cabin—or tried. Wardrobe malfunction. My flight suit, now tied off with the sleeves around my waist, had sagged, catching my leg. We locked eyes for a split second, and I couldn't help but laugh at the absurdity of the whole situation. ███ chuckled as he awkwardly grabbed the seat of my suit and pushed me over the edge of the bay door. Then he gave me another shove, and I half rolled across the floor, soaking up puddles of fuel. He clambered in behind me on the floor, both of us now laughing like idiots. TJ, holding guard from the front of the bird, turned around to see if we had cracked. Maybe we had a little, laughing that hard under these circumstances. It was just the tension breaker we needed, though.

Taliban fighters had now zeroed in on our big helicopter, and bullets were zipping across the rocks all around us. Despite the shots coming from all different directions, no one on our team had fired a weapon yet. Our rules of engagement said we needed positive identification. In this case, the rules made perfect sense. We might have let off some frustration firing wildly at the hills, only to waste ammunition we sorely needed to save for when the Taliban came for us in person. Without a clear point of origin for the enemy gunfire, there was no use in pulling the trigger, and we couldn't endanger possible civilians. The helos overhead couldn't see either— there were too many crags and caves up the hillside giving our enemy great cover.

Just then the radio crackled on the emergency channel. "Pedro one five, Shamus three four." It was one of the Kiowas. "Pedro one five, be advised we're RTB for refuel and rearm."

Goddammit—they're leaving us, too? Without air cover, the Taliban would overrun our little team within minutes. Their rockets were the only thing keeping the enemy at bay. The Kiowa pilot had to know that, because what he said next was crazy.

"If you can move your asses—fast—we'll swing by you first and take you out on our skids."

I looked over at TJ, who was hunched over the radio, to make sure I hadn't imagined it. On the skids? This was Afghanistan, not Hollywood. Kiowas do not land on the battlefield, and they do not carry pilots on their skids. Kiowas don't have extra seats, and they don't have enough power to handle the extra weight of passengers, especially not in this heat. *But maybe if they're light on fuel and ammo . . . And what about our patients?*

"Negative—there's too many of us—and we've got three patients."

"Copy that, Pedro one five," the Kiowa pilot said. "We'll have Pedro one six land to get your patients and PJs."

Finally. Our sister ship was going to land. The Kiowas would take four aircrew out on their skids first, and the rest would go with Pedro 16. This might just work.

"Aircrew out first," ▉▉▉▉ said. "MJ—you and the Gunner jump on the first Kiowa."

"No way," I protested. I didn't want to leave the others

behind. Then I bit my tongue. ███████ was the PJ team leader. Technically, George was in command, but he would never second-guess ███████ orders. Tactical lead had fallen to ███████ as soon as we had stopped flying and started acting like ground troops. He didn't need me second-guessing him just because I didn't want to evac first.

As much as I hated to leave my team behind, the sight of those two elegant Army choppers fluttering down to get us made me swoon. It was the most beautiful sight I had ever seen. I turned to ███████ and started stripping ammo magazines and water out of my survival vest. He needed it now more than I did.

"This is bullsh*t, man," I couldn't help noting. "I want to stay here with you guys until we can all get out."

George and I locked eyes. I could see he felt the exact same way, but we also both knew that the PJs took tactical lead in a ground scenario, and the best thing I could do for the group would be to do as I was told—not really a skill I was known for.

███████ laughed as he took my ammunition, nodding in appreciation of a fellow warrior.

"I'll see you at KAF," he said.

I swallowed my pride and turned toward the Army chopper, keeping one magazine on me just in case we had to make another unscheduled "landing" on the Kiowa. The other PJ clipped a lanyard into my belt with a carabiner so I could lash myself to the Kiowa's skids. It was going to be a bumpy ride.

Despite my wounds, I wasn't feeling any pain, just

adrenaline coursing through my body. I jogged out to the Kiowa with TJ, nodding at him as he pointed to the side of the aircraft he planned to jump on.

I wasn't thinking about it at the time, but I had left some of my gear behind, including my flag. I was about to go on a combat flight without my lucky charm for the first time in my career, but TJ and I had to travel light. Despite leaving our beautiful helo behind, I was glad to have TJ with me as we boarded our new one. We hunched under the spinning rotor blades and headed for opposite skids to keep the bird balanced. I planted my right foot on the skid, swung my left leg over to sit on the metal mount that led from the fuselage to the rocket pod, and leaned my back against the helo, bracing my rifle across the pod.

I glanced back at our broken bird as we prepared to lift off. The PJs had two of our patients out, preparing to make for our sister ship. Pedro 16 had just touched down about a hundred yards away—an eternity over the rocky terrain while also under fire. I counted the two PJs and the three patients—and then, goddammit, Steve holding up one end of the litter. He should have been lashed on to the other Kiowa.

I knew him well enough to know exactly what must have happened: He'd seen the PJs struggling to get two patients and a litter across the ridiculous amount of terrain that Pedro 16 had put between them and the wrecked aircraft. Seeing this, Steve had given up his one sure ticket out to help the PJs move the wounded across the open ground under steady Taliban sniper fire. I was furious at him for putting himself in danger, but at the same time, admiration flooded over me. Admiration and worry. I was also jealous that he'd managed to convince the PJs to let him stay while I was being forced to bug out.

I looped my lanyard around the rocket pod mount, then clipped it back into my belt. I slapped the fuselage twice to say "go," but the pilot was already beginning to lift the aircraft. Even a fearless chopper pilot like him didn't want to stay more than a moment down here. I heard the difference in the rotors as the Kiowa struggled under the extra weight of two passengers it wasn't designed for. I felt the lightening of the aircraft that meant we were about to take off.

Then all of my Christmases came at once. A tiny flame of light caught my attention from about seventy yards behind the crashed aircraft, at the Kiowa's two o'clock position. Looking down the sight of my rifle, braced across the rocket pod, I watched a Taliban fighter's muzzle flash, then flash again.

Finally. *Point of origin!* I wanted to scream victory into the rotor wash. It meant I finally had something to shoot at. I knew TJ couldn't have seen it, though, hanging on to the other skid, with the fuselage blocking his vision. I managed to squeeze off a dozen rounds as the helo lifted off the ground. I doubted my shots could be lethal or even accurate at this range. All I could hope for was to get the enemy to duck to give us enough time to take off. If I kicked up enough dust, there was a chance the others might be able to see where my shots were aimed so they could identify a point of origin for their own weapons.

I had no radio contact with the Kiowa pilot, though, so after a few rounds, I knew I couldn't keep firing. For all I knew, the other Kiowa was coming around or there were other friendly forces coming up. I had no choice but to save my remaining rounds in case I needed them again.

Then I had a thought that chilled me to the bone. The fact that I could finally see muzzle flashes might mean the Taliban, emboldened by the exfiltration attempt, had decided to abandon their dug-in position and move in to finish off the rest of our rescue team on the ground.

The twenty-minute flight to the nearest forward operating base felt like hours. The wind nearly thrashed my clothes off my body as I clung to the rocket pod for dear life, but the hardest part was not knowing if Steve and the PJs had made it out. Pedro 16 blew by us moments later, too fast for me to see if my brothers were aboard.

As I glanced back down to the terrain below us, the gale-force winds slowly inched my sunglasses out of my cargo pocket, and I watched them drop off into the ether. Lashed to the outside of the bird, gasping hot desert air at 130 knots, I was struck by the absurdity, and I laughed as my Oakleys whirled down to rest on Afghan earth. I pictured a peaceful ten-year-old Kandahari goat herder wearing them as he tended to his flock.

Twenty minutes later the Kiowa crossed back over the wire at a FOB called Frontenac. After dropping us there, the Kiowas would turn and burn, filling up on fuel and ammo, then head back to the crippled convoy. I had only one thing on my mind:

the fate of those I'd left behind. Before the skids even touched the runway, I unhooked and jumped off. I'm ashamed to say I never even turned to salute the brave Kiowa pilots who had just saved us—I was too desperate to find out about Steve and the others.

———— ● ————

I marched from the LZ onto the base, barely registering the horrified looks of the other soldiers milling around. I must have been a sight in my fuel-soaked body armor, blood crusted along my arm and down my leg, the arms of my flight suit still tied around my waist, rifle at the ready, helmet still on. Adrenaline still pumped through me even though I was back inside the wire.

A soldier stepped in my path. He had a square jaw covered with five-o'clock shadow.

"Move! I've got to get to the TOC," I demanded. I was aiming for the Tactical Operations Center, marked by the telltale flagpoles, where satellite feeds and radios would tell me if our team had survived.

The soldier in front of me was opening a trauma kit. Then I saw his blue latex gloves: The Kiowa pilots must have radioed ahead that they had an injured pilot tied to their skids. I ignored him and kept walking. The medic, caught off guard, stumbled backward in front of me. Only then did I notice TJ at my side. Had he been walking along with me since the landing?

"Captain . . . Captain, sir, I have to check out these

TieJie "TJ" Jones (on right).

wounds. I can't let you go until I take a look," the medic insisted.

I ignored the "sir" and kept walking, but he continued to shuffle backward in front of me and TJ. Without breaking stride, I switched my rifle to my left hand and showed him my right arm.

"See? I'm fine. Little shrapnel, but it's small, and I can get it out later."

"Okay," he persisted annoyingly, "but I'm going to have to take a look at that leg."

Exasperated, I stopped. If the medic was going to get in my way, he'd better make it quick. I looked him in the eye and dropped my pants right there in the middle of the yard. A dozen or so soldiers had been watching our awkward dance toward the TOC, but until that moment I'm not sure they noticed I was a woman under all of that body armor and helmet. Now they stared openly—at my Hello Kitty panties.

TJ stepped up to the nearest soldier and nearly blew him down. "What the F**K are YOU looking at?"

All of the men snapped out of their stasis and urgently rediscovered whatever activities they had been doing before my arrival. The medic dropped to his knees, seizing his chance to look at my leg wound.

"Okay—no more bleeding. You're good to go . . . ma'am."

Satisfied that I wasn't in any immediate mortal danger, the medic let me keep walking, but still he danced alongside us while pulling out some pills.

"A painkiller and some antibiotics," he said, thrusting the tablets out to me.

"No way. No dope. If our team isn't out, I'm going back to get them."

"I get that, ma'am, but at least take this antibiotic. You've got foreign body material embedded in your arm and leg. You don't know what was on that bullet."

Point taken. I grabbed the pill he handed to me, dry swallowing it with a quick gulp.

He sheepishly rubbed his stubbled chin, displayed a coy victory smile, and produced another tablet.

"Actually, *this* one's the antibiotic."

I nearly slugged him. I hadn't needed a painkiller. The wounds didn't hurt; the only pain came from not knowing about the others. If they hadn't made it back to base, I needed to be alert enough to go back out to get them. Of course they had plenty of other crews, and I wouldn't be allowed to fly again until after the debrief, but that didn't register with me at the time. I'd steal one of their trucks to get back out there if I had to.

I reached the plywood door to the TOC and threw it open. It squealed shut behind me and TJ. A few eyes glanced up at us, but then went straight back down to their work—they had a convoy under fire and a rescue bird down, after all. There were more important things to focus on than visitors.

"How can we help you, ma'am?" said the soldier closest to the door, without looking away from his screen.

"I only need a second, soldier. I'm Pedro one five, and I need to know the status of my patients and remaining crew."

Everyone looked up at once in surprise, sizing up TJ and me with a stare. No one spoke, and I felt a shiver—what did they know that I didn't? Had they been listening to our team radio for help as they were overrun by Taliban?

The door squealed again as George walked in behind us. He'd arrived on the other Kiowa skid and looked as anxious as I felt.

"Hey, did Steve and our PJs get out okay?" George asked.

A captain whose uniform looked a little too clean stood up from behind his plywood desk.

"Everyone made it," he said.

Three beautiful words.

I couldn't wait to hug Steve, and then I couldn't wait to punch him.

NINE

WHEN WE GOT BACK to Kandahar after the incident, I walked toward the TOC with my gear, minus my flag and the other things I had left in the aircraft, as I always had. But something had changed. The pro super (short for "production superintendent," the person in charge of the flightline maintainers) ran out to meet me. From my years as a maintenance officer, I knew that these guys loved each aircraft like the classic car you keep in your garage under a tarp. They knew the quirks and ticks that made each one unique, and Aircraft 118, which we had just left in the desert full of holes and drenched in fuel, was one of the best.

"Sh*t," I greeted him. "I'm so sorry about 118 and all the work you guys just put into her windshield."

He was stunned; his jaw dropped for a moment. Then he snapped out of it and gave me a big hug, gear and all.

"Are you f**king kidding me? I'm so happy to see you. Are you guys okay?"

The full impact of what had happened clearly still hadn't hit me. Of course he cared more about us than the aircraft we'd left behind, but for some reason my mind was still in high-alert warrior mode, and until I could switch it off, I couldn't quite comprehend just how close we had come to getting killed or captured.

The pro super started walking back with me toward the TOC, helping me carry some of my gear. When I looked up, I saw some brass heading my way. Luckily it wasn't Colonel Johnson this time, but I could tell it was someone important from the number of people surrounding him. As he got closer, I could see the stars on his uniform and realized it was the base commander.

"Captain!" he shouted as he drew closer. "Are you MJ?"

"Yes, sir," I replied. I really didn't want to do this now. *Can I at least put down my gear and wash some of the fuel out of the holes in my arm?*

He reached his right hand out and aggressively pumped my arm up and down, clearly excited that he wouldn't have to write a letter home to my loved ones.

"Hey, I thought you got shot. Is all of this your blood?" he asked. "Where did you take a round?" He peppered me with questions as he continued to shake the arm that had been shredded by the shrapnel.

His hand still gripping mine, I twisted our hands around to show him my forearm wounds.

"This is where I took most of the damage, but . . ."

He jerked his hand away as if he had burned it on a hot pan.

"Uhh, it's mostly superficial. It doesn't hurt that bad," I finished awkwardly, amused by the pained look on his face.

I couldn't help but stifle a laugh—vigorously shaking the wounded arm of a pilot who had just been shot was a pretty good faux pas to make in front of his entourage.

"Well, at least you're a good clotter." He chuckled.

There was an embarrassed pause. This was obviously not going the way he had envisioned it. I decided to try to lighten the moment.

"Nah. I cauterized the wounds with the cigar I was smoking at the time," I retorted.

Everyone laughed, but it was the kind of laugh where they weren't entirely sure I was kidding. I kept walking, continuing my journey into the TOC for the debrief.

Traditionally no one outside of the crew was allowed into the debrief, so that the crew could feel free to be completely honest about every aspect of the flight, including all of the screwups. But when I walked into the TOC, it was clear that this time would be different.

Usually there are only about five or ten people in the twenty-by-forty-foot TOC at a time. That day I was surprised to see about fifty people milling around, waiting to hear about what had happened to us five hours earlier. Rhys made a bee-line for me and gave me a big hug. He had once told me I was like a little sister to him, and the look in his eyes when he said it showed me that he wasn't bullsh*tting me.

"Man, I'm f**king glad to see you," he said. I think it's the first and last time I ever heard him drop an F-bomb.

I had a moment to consider the toll it had taken on him, as our commander, having the friends he carried responsibility for in such great peril. As I looked around the room at the brass, intel folks, the chaplain, and many others I'd never met before, I wondered how open everyone would be about the things that had gone wrong, given the expanded audience. I saw a couple of Army uniforms and hoped these were my Kiowa pilots so I might get a chance to thank them. I wouldn't have time to find out, though, as the debrief got under way immediately.

It was packed in the room—standing room only. Still, I was pretty surprised when the few seats that were available weren't offered up to the exhausted, fuel-soaked crew. I looked down at my bloody uniform, dry but giving off fuel vapors, and figured that was why people were staring at me. George, as Flight Lead, cleared his throat and began.

"Okay, so we stepped to the aircraft without any problems; run-up and taxi were standard. We got some reports from intel over the radio about the ongoing threat and to expect the Kiowas on scene."

He continued from there, and for the most part, it was a standard debrief. Other than the exceptional details and the audience, it was just like any other. I grew worried as we got to the end, thinking that some of our decisions would be questioned. While I think we did the best we could at the time with the information we had, you could make the case that we never should have gone back in the second time.

Some would argue that we should have waited for the

A-10s to get on scene, but we had three urgent American medevac patients down there, and we had reason to believe the round I had taken was just a lucky shot. No one mentioned the fact that Pedro 16 refused to go into the zone.

When George and Pedro 16's Aircraft Commander got to the part where we were isolated on the ground, the other AC chimed in and started making claims that I was not willing to let slide.

"Then we all landed to pick you guys up," he said, clearing his throat.

"Wait a minute," I piped up.

Fifty faces turned to me. About five of them already knew what I was going to say, and from the looks on their faces, they were relieved someone was going to call him on his bullsh*t.

Do it, MJ. Someone has to say something.

"Why did it take you guys so long to pick us up?" I questioned him straight to his face. "Were you dumping gas? I would have thought you guys would have landed right next to us as soon as we shut down."

The AC stared at me in disbelief. The silence was deafening.

"You weren't on the ground that long," he snapped back. "Anyway, at that point—"

"No," I interrupted him. "We were. We were there for, like, twenty minutes!"

"I'm sure it felt like that, MJ." He chuckled, as if he were talking to a child. "But it wasn't long at all."

"Intel . . . how long were we on the ground?"

Throughout the entire incident, the intel guys and gals

had been listening to the radios and taking note of every single thing that happened, including the times.

"Um, eighteen minutes, Captain," the intel troop answered sheepishly. It was clear he did not want to get in the middle of this.

"Eighteen minutes." I nodded confidently. "Okay, so what took eighteen minutes?"

Eighteen minutes was a *long* f**king time to be sitting on the ground taking fire when a perfectly good aircraft was circling above, refusing to land.

"I don't know," he said.

I looked at the Kiowa pilots, who were elbowing each other and sort of shaking their heads. The truth was, and we all knew it, that we would *still* be there waiting if it hadn't been for the Kiowa pilots. It wasn't until they landed, showing 16 it was safe, and thereby taking tactical lead away from Pedro 16, that they had finally been forced into action.

"Okay, so at that point the Kiowas landed," I went on, satisfied that I had made my point and ready for the debrief to continue.

"Right," said George, as he continued with a pleased smirk.

Next they got to the part in the timeline where I fired my weapon. I did feel I had positive identification of the enemy and a solid point of origin, but I wasn't on comm with the Kiowa pilots, so I easily could have put the other aircraft in danger if he had been maneuvering into my firing line. It was less than ideal, to say the least, and now it would be time for me to take my lumps. Pedro 16's AC gave me a smug smile, knowing what was probably coming, happy that I was on the receiving end this time.

But George just breezed over the fact that I had been firing and began to ask the room if there were any questions. I couldn't believe it. The debrief was nearly over, and I was about to get away clean. Then one of the Army guys raised his hand.

"Who was it that was firing off of my skid?" he asked.

Sh*t. I was going to be in so much trouble. I had let my protective instinct for Steve and the others cloud my judgment, and I'd probably be grounded for it. So much for my flying career.

I took a deep breath and meekly raised my hand to the level of my ear.

"Umm, that was me."

"F**kin' A, that was awesome," he responded with a grin. "We were out of ammo, and when I saw that muzzle flash, I didn't think we were going to make it outta there. You got their heads down so we could lift. Nice job."

"Thanks," I said, looking at Rhys to see whether or not I'd get in trouble. He read my mind and smiled reassuringly. No one questioned whether or not I should have squeezed that trigger. Thank goodness I had.

The chaplain stepped up and announced that he was available if any of us needed to "talk to someone." We looked at one another and sort of chuckled. No thanks. We'd pass. Especially since we weren't about to raise a hand in front of fifty people.

As the meeting broke up, Rhys approached me to take a look at my arm. I could see in his eyes that he had taken the stress of what had happened harder than any of us; he almost looked as if he was going to tear up. He was the squadron commander at the time, and we were his responsibility.

"MJ, you need to go get that arm checked out," he said, skipping emotions for logistics.

I didn't tell him that it was my back that hurt the most. Something about the way we had landed had knocked my back out of alignment, and I had a bad feeling that it was going to catch up to me sooner rather than later.

I walked out of the TOC, hearing Rhys in the background arranging for someone to drive me to the hospital as the door closed. It was only about five P.M., still too damn hot for my liking, but I was too happy to be at KAF to care. I knew I was incredibly lucky to be there instead of in the back of some Taliban pickup truck with a hood over my head on my way to a basement somewhere in Marjah. I heard the door to the TOC swing open and close behind me, and I turned around to see Doug Sherry standing there, looking past me to the taxiway with the stub of his cigar between his teeth.

I waited to see if he would either ignore me, as he had done so many times before, or tell me all of the things I did wrong.

"Hey, Doug," I said, steeling myself for either outcome.

He took a good twenty seconds before finally looking at me. He looked down at his boots for a tick, kicked a rock around a bit, and then, appearing to come to some sort of a decision, he looked at me.

"You did good, kid."

I stood there, stunned. The rest of his crew filed out of the TOC after him, and he followed them out to the gate as they headed to chow. Long after they were out of sight, I was still standing there dumbstruck. It wasn't much, but it was the best validation of my actions I could hope for. That acknowledgment, from a pilot of his caliber, especially considering our complicated history, meant more to me than all the medals they would pin on my chest in the days to come.

I begrudgingly let someone drive me to the hospital. They took X-rays, plucked a few of the shrapnel pieces out, then flushed the holes with saline. An hour later I was back in the TOC, ready to get back to work. Once it was clear that they wouldn't let us fly again that day, my crew and I retreated to the gazebo covered in Christmas lights. We weren't ready to go back to our rooms just yet. Something still felt unfinished.

Sitting there watching the sun set, smelling the sh*t pond, we took turns with the lighter as we fired up our cigars. I took the one I had been saving out of my survival vest, figuring now was as good a time as any to celebrate. Who knew if I'd get another chance?

We all laughed together at the obvious danger of smoking cigars while covered in fuel on top of a wooden gazebo, but at that point, most of us felt pretty invincible. I would say bulletproof, but that had clearly been disproven.

"Hey, Steve, I bet even you could get laid using this story in a bar," one of the guys joked. The full-bellied laughter that ensued was more cathartic and better therapy than anything the chaplain could have said to us. We were punch-drunk and thrilled to be alive, to be together, and to be ribbing Steve. When I look back and miss my days flying with my "family," this is the memory that pulls the hardest.

———— • ————

Later that night, the PJs went back in to pick up the PJ we had left at the convoy. None of us could go back to our rooms until we knew he was safe, but we'd be in for a wait. George headed into a porta potty to do some business. I was cleaning my rifle in the aircrew locker end of the TOC, near the porta potties outside the back door, when I heard a commotion.

"Holy sh*t!"

The plastic door banged open, followed by the back door to the TOC, and then a very excited George stormed in.

"Are you okay?" I asked. Now that some of the adrenaline had passed, I was a little worried about all of us. We were sort of guardrail-to-guardrail emotionally, so I wondered what had George so worked up.

"I took part of that round!" he said.

"You mean in your vest?"

When we had inspected our gear after arriving back at KAF, George had noticed that part of the round had hit his body armor and lodged in his survival-gear vest. The shrapnel had impacted his flare, which, if it had gone off, would have been an added complication we really didn't need. We had all said a silent thank-you to the universe that it hadn't.

"NO!" he said. "I just pulled a piece of it out of my thigh!"

Luckily, the shrapnel hadn't gone in very deep, so he hadn't bled much, but it was still unnerving to pull part of a bullet out of your body. He'd have to go get it checked out just in case, but he was okay.

I knew how he felt. I had already used the tip of my pocketknife to pull out about five pieces, and over the next couple of days I would pull out about ten more as they made their way to the surface. I tried to do it where no one could see me, as it made people squeamish. But I couldn't stop looking for it, waiting for more to appear. There was something that made me angry about carrying around all that enemy metal.

Before the night was over, the PJs brought home their brother safe and sound, and we started trying to get back to business as usual. As our commander, Rhys had been trying his hardest to get the Canadians in the area to drop some munitions on our abandoned aircraft to destroy any classified equipment on board, but he couldn't get any help. On the Predator feed, we had already seen a Taliban truck carrying parts away, and I knew Rhys felt defeated as he watched it. He had done everything he could to keep the aircraft out of enemy hands, but there it was on the screen, being hauled away one piece at a time. It was a terrible feeling, and we didn't want to let more of our sensitive equipment fall into the wrong hands. Technically, we should have pulled some of that equipment out when we were rescued, but we'd had to travel light, and it was the very last thing any of us were thinking about.

Over the next few days, the Army and Air Force collaborated to try to get our aircraft out. The crash recovery team had a plan to bring in a large Chinook helicopter with dual rotors and the ability to cargo-sling out our heavy bird. A few of our maintainers volunteered to join the effort to make sure 118 was well taken care of.

Honestly, I was mainly looking forward to getting a good assessment of the damage. The number of systems we had lost and the number of holes she had withstood had to be some kind of record. Unfortunately we would never find out.

To sling 118 out, they would need to saw off her rotors. The book called for this to be done one at a time, rotating each blade around to the nose of the aircraft, but our guys knew they were in bad-guy territory and, understandably, wanted to expedite. So instead they were cutting them off as quickly as possible, without rotating them around to the nose. As they cut the blades off the sides, the sparks they generated landed on the substantial amount of fuel still covering the cargo bay. Suddenly, the entire aircraft was on fire.

Our maintainers had only a moment to stare in shock at the burning aircraft. Before the whole helicopter was engulfed, one of the maintainers actually managed to reach into the cockpit to grab the bag I had left behind, the one holding the flag I had carried with me on every single combat mission I had ever flown. I will be forever in his debt for saving it from the ensuing inferno. When he returned it to me, a little charred and melted around the edge, I threw my arms around him and squeezed him as hard as I could. My hero.

At the end of that deployment, when the next group came in to replace us, one of their young pilots stopped me in passing in the TOC.

"Hey . . . what was your call sign? We're trying to think of one for us."

"Pedro. We were Pedro." And we were. I was so proud. We had lived up to the name. We would always be Pedro.

"Pedro? Why, are you guys near Mexico?"

I just chuckled and walked away. He'd figure it out.

I found out later that the incoming squadron kept our name. Apparently we had built quite a reputation with the American and international ground forces. There were many different platforms that could be tapped to pull out someone who was injured on the battlefield, but when ground forces heard the name "Pedro" on the radio, their spirits were lifted because they knew we would get them out at all costs.

As of 2015, six years later, Pedro was still being used by each incoming rescue squadron. We had earned the Pedro call sign on that deployment, and I finally felt like I had earned the right to walk the halls with the rescue heroes I so admired.

———— • ————

Our return trip back to the States was more fun than I'd thought possible. We stopped over at Diego Garcia, a horseshoe-shaped island reef in the middle of the Indian Ocean with a small military presence. We had nothing to do but drink and celebrate the fact that we were all still alive.

The afternoon started out tame enough, with a few of us mixing a cocktail or two. But things went downhill when one of the Gunners started giving everyone what he called "naked Gunner hugs." You would get a hug and a slurred "I love you" over your shoulder until, in the spirit of camaraderie, you'd pat his arm and say, "I love you, too." Then you realized that he had dropped his drawers to his ankles. It's easy to see how this could spiral into something bad, but there in Diego Garcia, it was like someone had opened a release valve and let the pressure out of the group; I knew that even though I was the only woman, I had obtained equal status with these hugs (and that if I had been uncomfortable, my objections would have been met with an anguished apology). But I wasn't uncomfortable. We loved each other, we truly did, and we had just survived one of the craziest deployments any of us had ever known.

As the afternoon progressed, we invariably ended up looking out over the ocean. More and more of us accumulated out there, slightly inebriated, until there were probably twenty of us standing in the sand, wiggling our toes in the water. I heard some snickering over my shoulder, and I looked down the beach about ten feet to my right to see a sight that would be burned into my retinas forever. Doug Sherry, in his tightywhities, taking off running toward the water, the stub of his cigar still clenched between his teeth.

After spending four months covered in sand and dirt in

Pedro 15.

the heat of the desert, suddenly the thought of jumping into the Indian Ocean was the greatest idea any of us had ever heard. We all instantly stripped and followed Doug into the water. The ocean was warm and welcoming; I never wanted to get out again. That swim, which I'll remember forever, was both physically and emotionally cleansing. It should be a required activity for every person reintegrating into civilization straight from the violence and horror of the battlefield.

———— ◆ ————

After our brief tropical interlude in Diego Garcia, it was time to get back to real life. Once we had arrived stateside, reality hit, and it hit some of us harder than others. Coming home

TOP: *MJ and* ▮▮▮▮▮▮.
ABOVE: *Steven, George, MJ, and* ▮▮▮▮▮▮.

to our families and facing the mundane indignities of ordinary life (like paying bills and filing tax returns) can be difficult after the time spent at war.

Some people have a hard time coming home to find that everything went on as usual without them. Kids played sports and went to school and made new friends. Spouses filled up their cars with gas and went grocery shopping and chatted on the phone while we were trading fire with a skilled and determined enemy and were busy rescuing young men and women with missing limbs who were bleeding out in the back of our aircraft.

It is no one's fault, but it is surreal being reinserted into this world of complacence and monotony as if nothing had happened. You have to reach deep down inside yourself and turn off that survival-mode switch. Some of us are better at this than others.

When we got back, I took some time off and visited my mom in Austin, Texas. I was doing okay, but I would sometimes wake up in the middle of the night in a sweat. I wasn't dreaming about getting shot down, though. For me the thing that was difficult to recover from was the actual medevac missions and the fact that we couldn't save everyone. I can barely recall any of the times we saved people, which was more often than not, but when I look back at my missions, it's the ones I lost that usually come to mind. Did I do everything I could? Could I have gotten to them faster?

Shortly after my return home, I started being short-tempered with people who would complain about things like waiting for their check at a restaurant. I no longer enjoyed watching horror movies or military movies. The first movie I saw after returning home was *Tropic Thunder*. It's a hilarious movie, but it opens with a scene where they are filming a Vietnam-era war movie and a character has his guts spilling out. I had to walk out of the theater. It was too real, and I didn't have it in me to find it funny. I had seen far worse things in real life, but watching it on a screen also made me feel guilty that I was watching a movie while some people would never return to their loved ones. The gory images, used for entertainment and humor, were just too much for me to handle.

Once I was back home again, surrounded by the monotony of everyday life, I started pushing back, hard, against the tedium. My lifelong addiction to adrenaline started to look like it was going to get me killed. My brain's chemistry had reset the bar for what was thrilling and death-defying—my level was now set at shoot-downs in enemy territory—so I started looking for thrills anywhere I could find them. I found myself driving my motorcycle harder, faster, and tighter around corners. I went skydiving. Nothing I tried could get me that high I'd become addicted to. This was ridiculous, and I recognized that if I kept notching up the ante, eventually I'd go too far. I had to make a change.

In the spring of 2010, I was sent to Aircraft Commander Upgrade training at Kirtland AFB in Albuquerque. I did well, as I always had in training, so they fast-tracked me to the end. But when I returned to my squadron as an Aircraft Commander, a cold reality began to settle in. I knew I was a good pilot, but I felt the full weight of my new responsibility. As the AC, I would be in charge of an aircraft full of people. My decisions would be life and death, for my patients as well as my crew. I needed to be at the top of my game, both physically, as a pilot, and psychologically, as a leader. I owed that to my crew.

Here's the thing about PTSD. It's been my experience that everyone coming home from a war zone who went outside the wire and saw actual combat has some degree of post-traumatic stress. I don't know whether every person reaches what I would call "disorder" level, as I'm not a psychologist. I will say that my squadron mates seemed willing and even eager to share their struggles with me, whether it was trouble at home, ceaseless nightmares, short fuses, or finding themselves easily startled. I had always heard that getting help for this type of thing would ruin your career, but there were so many of us suffering (myself included) that I thought if I were half the leader I hoped to be, I should set the example and get some help.

Unfortunately, instead of others taking my lead, they would corner me and ask me what my counselor had told me. It was as if there was a magic recipe to get over what we had experienced, and they thought I could pass on the secrets I'd learned from my own therapy.

"Hey, can you ask her what it means if you keep having a nightmare that a tiger is chasing you through a supermarket?" a friend asked me while we were chatting in a hallway one afternoon.

We all had issues; we just dealt with them differently. When I see a report suggesting that women get PTSD more often than men, I have to wonder how much of that data is skewed by the fact that we might be more likely to admit we need some help. And shouldn't that be a good thing?

A few months after I'd returned home, I informed my chain of command that I was going to quit my full-time job. As of May 2010, I would no longer be a Team Hawk pilot. I wanted to move home to Austin to become a "Traditional Guardsman." I would go to California for training, but I would be commuting in from Austin instead of living in California and working there full-time.

Finn thought I was crazy. The job I held was coveted by most of the pilots I knew, and he thought I would regret leaving. As close as we were, he didn't know me as well as I knew myself. It was time for a change. I just didn't know how I would tell Steve.

"Whaaaaat? Why?" Steve asked when I told him of my plans.

"I don't know. I miss Austin, and I feel like it's just time for a change. I never wanted to do twenty years, you know," I told him. "I love this job, but you gotta admit, it's a sh*tty environment. We all have to hide our injuries from the flight doc, and we live in fear of being disqualified if we admit to having nightmares. Aren't you sick of that?"

He shrugged, revealing nothing.

"Besides, I can't stand coming to work and seeing your ugly mug every day," I finished with a grin.

I could tell he was disappointed, but of course he retorted with something equally offensive. Then we did that macho slap-hug thing we always did and left it at that. I knew we would see each other again and that no matter where each of us moved, we'd remain close. Even if months or years went by without talking, I knew we would always fall back into the easy, insult-trading banter that had marked our entire friendship. I might be leaving Team Hawk behind, but some of my brothers and sisters, I hoped, would remain part of my family for life.

———— • ————

A few weeks after Steve and I had talked, I moved home to Austin. It was time to start thinking about my next chapter. I was thirty-four years old, unattached, and trying to figure out what I wanted to be when I grew up. There were so many civilian careers I could try out! I could buy a house and plant some roots without fear of being ordered to move. It was an exciting time, but it was about to get infinitely better.

I arrived home in the middle of a blazing-hot Texan summer in 2010. After about a week, I was eager to reconnect with some of my friends from my childhood, so I agreed to meet a few of them out for drinks. I was conflicted about going to a Podunk bar in Leander, Texas, as opposed to some hip joint downtown on Sixth Street, but this is where I came from. This was home. Despite feeling like I had escaped from the small town I'd grown up in and accomplished so much, I never wanted to let myself feel like I was too good for Leander.

On a sultry August night, my engine rumbled as I pulled my purple Dodge Challenger, a deployment gift to myself, into the parking lot of a strip mall and looked around for the sign. Spotting the bar, I tried not to roll my eyes. It was a classic run-down dive bar, but I was excited to see my friends, so I jumped out of the car and walked inside. It was around seven P.M., so it didn't take me long to spot my group, as there were only about a dozen people in there at this hour.

After a round of hugs and happy greetings, we quickly fell into a long, comfortable conversation about what we had all been up to. Someone mentioned that they were in touch with Brandon Hegar, the drum major of our high school's band, and that he'd be joining us shortly. Of course I remembered Brandon—he had been in my class in high school. I distantly remembered that all the girls in the band had had a crush on him. He was just that kind of guy—sweet and funny and popular.

I was at the bar ordering a round of drinks when I heard the door swing open. I turned over my left shoulder to see who had walked in. A tall, handsome man was striding into the bar. I jerked my head back around to the bartender so I wouldn't get caught staring.

It had to be Brandon, but he was way hotter than I remembered. Standing six feet tall and carrying a brawny 180 pounds, he had really grown up from the high school kid I had known.

He had a light brown faux hawk and a manicured beard that gave him kind of a Joshua-Jackson-meets-David-Beckham vibe.

"One more beer, please," I asked the bartender as I watched Brandon saunter over to my friends to hug everyone. I walked back to the table with my arms full of beers, and our eyes met. His crystal-blue eyes made my heart skip a beat.

What the hell is wrong with me? Am I still in high school?

"Hi," I said stupidly. I was never very good at this sort of thing, and I was way out of practice. "You're Brandon, right? How've you been?"

We kept chatting as we nursed our drinks, and everyone else seemed to slowly fade into the blurry background. It felt great to be a normal person again, just sipping beers and making small talk, but it was more than that. Granted, I had had a few Irish Car Bombs, but it was crazy how quickly I felt like I had met my other half.

Sure enough, though, eventually he asked me what I had been doing since high school. I'd been dreading the topic, but I'd known it would come up. Experience had taught me that one of two things would happen at this point. I would tell him I was a pilot and he would either get intimidated and become disinterested, or he'd get excited and want to talk to me all about rates of fire, engine horsepower, and confirmed kills. I couldn't help but feel like I was always either just one of the guys or too "strong" of a woman, making a guy feel like less of a man because his job wasn't as tough or something equally stupid.

I looked down at my drink and tried to enjoy the last

moments of talking to this funny, gorgeous guy before having to find out which one he'd choose. Finally I couldn't dodge the question anymore, and I told him about my job. His beautiful blue eyes widened.

"Really? That's f**king awesome!" he said. Okay, now it was time for the barrage of technical questions. To my delight, he surprised me with a completely different response.

"Man, that's hot."

My smile widened. What do you know? There's a third option!

The next night was our first date, and we've been together ever since. Contrary to my previous belief, I discovered that a soul mate was actually a real thing, and I had found mine. The prospect of falling in love didn't scare me. His three kids from a previous marriage didn't scare me. His volatile ex-wife didn't scare me. I didn't care what I had to put up with; I was going to marry that man.

As it turned out, his kids are amazing, and I quickly fell just as in love with them. And to my utter delight, his dad reminded me of my dad and welcomed me into his family with open arms. With every new thing I learned about Brandon, I was more and more shocked that he was single. The previous year his wife had cheated on him, and boy oh boy, her loss was my gain. Some people just can't see a good thing when it's standing right in front of them. I wasted no time taking him off the market, and I felt luckier than I had the day we survived being shot down in Afghanistan. We'd met in late August and were engaged to be married by Christmas.

In the months that we had been dating, I had been flying back and forth from California, working as a part-time pilot. Even though I was only flying part-time, I still needed to be at 100 percent. My knee was doing okay, but my back was in constant pain. Luckily, after the rough recovery I'd had from my knee surgery, I had been granted a waiver to be able to do the run portion of my physical fitness test on a treadmill instead of on asphalt, as the absence of cartilage made it hard to run on hard surfaces.

Unfortunately, the back injury I had suffered in the crash hadn't healed; in fact, just the opposite. Afraid of getting grounded, I hadn't gotten any medical attention for it, and it was getting worse and worse.

With all of this at the forefront of my mind, I went on my first temporary duty (TDY) for a week-long exercise with my squadron as an Aircraft Commander in October 2010. We flew from our home base at Moffett Federal Airfield just outside San Jose, California, down to an Army base called Fort Hunter Liggett. At Hunter Liggett, there is a kick-ass live-ammo gun range. It was the closest we could come to the real thing for practice, rolling in and firing at mock enemy positions while rescuing simulated survivors. I had a blast until one of the last flights at the end of the exercise.

I was flying with Finn, my friend who'd hired me and was the Team Hawk commander at the time. We came in to land at a simulated pickup of a patient, and when the wheels touched down, I heard a crack-of-the-bat sound and saw the windshield in front of me spiderweb out.

I blinked and shook my head a little, and when I looked up again, the windshield was fine. I looked down at my arm and leg, but saw no blood. I looked over at Finn, and he just stared at me.

"Hey . . . you okay?"

"Fine. I'm fine," I replied a little too quickly.

I was slightly rattled, but I was okay. It was so real, though. That was the first actual flashback I'd had—and it was very different from just a bad memory. I had experienced the exact moment that enemy round had blazed through my windshield all over again, and for some reason the flashback was almost worse than the real thing.

At the end of that exercise we landed back home at Moffett in California. As I was carrying my gear into the aircrew locker room, I heard someone calling my name. It was Finn, catching up to me with some bad news. Because of my time in training and the fact that I had been commuting in from Austin, I was overdue on my physical fitness test.

My flight home to Austin left the next morning, so despite being mentally and physically exhausted from the exercise we had just completed, I would need to retake it immediately. With no advance notice, though, I couldn't get a copy of my waiver from the medical group for the test proctor. When I asked if I could just take it when I came back in a few weeks, the answer was a firm no. Not wanting to make things difficult for my leadership, I begrudgingly took the test without the waiver. What was the worst that could happen, right?

I found out. Halfway through the 1.5-mile run, my knee exploded in pain. I stopped in my tracks, conscious of the fact I was being timed, and tested it by putting my foot on the ground. It felt okay, so I tried again. Nope. I was done. As my knee doubled in size, the test proctor drove me to the med group for assessment.

"Why were you running on asphalt if you have a waiver?" they asked me.

I just shook my head at the stupidity of it all.

On my way out of the medical group, I bumped into my flight doc, who was the person assigned to our squadron with the authority to decide who could fly and who was grounded.

"No problem," she told me. All I had to do was get an MRI on my knee and she could clear me to fly. I flew home, saw an orthopedic surgeon who also lectured me for running on asphalt, got an MRI, and returned to Moffett the next month expecting to be cleared. After all, I had done what was asked of me, right?

"Sh*t, MJ," the flight doc began. "I can't clear you to fly with your knee like this!"

"WHAT? You told me to get the MRI and I'd be clear. It's back to normal, so what's the problem?"

She just looked at me like I was crazy.

"I meant you needed a clean MRI. Did you know you have no cartilage in your knee?"

I nodded with a blank look on my face, trying to hide my fury.

*No sh*t, Sherlock. Maybe next time they'll believe me when I say*

I have a waiver and stop acting like I just don't want to run outside and mess up my hair.

She refused to clear me to fly. I flew back to Austin, disappointed, growing more and more frustrated over the amount of red tape I had to deal with.

Over the next few months, an argument between me, my chain of command, my flight doc, and her chain of command would ensue. The conclusion they reached was the most ridiculous thing I had ever heard. They would clear me to fly, but I would have to pass a test that they had made up on the spot. They wanted me to dress in full gear and show I could run on the taxiway six hundred yards away from an aircraft to simulate an aircraft with live ammunition that was on fire, in order to prove that I could get away from it to a safe distance.

"Are you kidding me?" I sputtered in response. "Didn't I just prove in Afghanistan that I can run away from a disabled aircraft?"

My real-world experience didn't matter as much as their simulated environment test. Typical military. Didn't they care that they were asking me to injure my knee again? At what point would reinjuring my knee and hiding my back injury have a permanent, long-term impact on my health? The ludicrous test they proposed was the last straw for me. They clearly couldn't see the big picture, and I wasn't going to continue to subject myself to permanent injury so that they could feel better about letting me fly.

Sometimes when fate is screaming at you, you have to listen. Now that I had met Brandon and experienced what real happiness felt like, suddenly the thought of being grounded no longer seemed like the end of the world. Perhaps it was finally time to close this chapter of my life and start another. Almost every person I had flown with was hiding some sort of illness or injury, but I was growing tired of that game. It was time to just let nature run its course.

It wasn't the way I had envisioned my career ending. I thought of the celebrations and "fini-flights" a lot of pilots have at the end of their time in the sky. I wouldn't get that opportunity. As strange as it sounds, for someone who had spent her entire life dreaming of being a pilot, my flying career ended without much of a bang.

I knew I was finished, but I also knew I had some fight left in me. So before I even flew back to Austin, I started looking for other ways in which I could serve my country and utilize the skills I had honed over the years as a pilot. I did some research and found out that there was, in fact, a job in which you needed iron resolve in combat, a good sense of the battle-field, and a solid understanding of the unique language and shorthand we use on the radios. I was thrilled—I could be a Special Tactics Officer and forward deploy with ground forces, calling in their airstrikes and ensuring there was no miscommunication that could result in friendly losses or civilian casualties. This job was right up my alley.

Except I wasn't allowed to even apply for it. The job was not open to women because there was an antiquated policy on the books called the Ground Combat Exclusion Policy, which was intended to keep women out of combat. The policy was news to me and to the deep scars on my right arm and leg, and I chuckled while thinking about the combat I had seen and the clear, direct ground combat I had medevaced other women out of in Afghanistan. That didn't seem fair to me, but I racked it up as the Air Force's loss. Their ridiculous and antiquated policies on job qualification meant they were about to lose a combat-seasoned warrior.

TEN

BACK HOME IN AUSTIN, Texas, I took on a consulting job for a hospital system. I had just married Brandon, and together we bought a beautiful house on half an acre. I was still coming to terms with the end of my flying career, however. I was trying to leave all thoughts of the military behind me as fond memories, but I would soon be pulled back in. In a thinly veiled attempt to bond with me—which I was thrilled about—my eldest stepdaughter, who was twelve at the time, told me she wanted to be a Marine one day. I was secretly over the moon at the thought of her picking a goal that would keep her out of trouble in her youth, just like mine did. I joked with her that she had better start doing some push-up training if she wanted to be a Marine, and we both dropped into front-leaning rest, giggling as we did our push-ups.

A few weeks later, she came to me in tears.

"Why did you let me think I could be a Marine?" she asked, clearly thinking I had made a fool of her.

I was at a loss. What could she possibly mean?

"My mom told me that I can't be a Marine because that's a boy's job."

That was it. I had really had it with people like this. I had spent my whole life putting up with people treating me like serving your country was a boy's job, whether it was because of their own insecurity or just plain ignorance.

I couldn't believe that this little girl would grow up in the same type of world as I had twenty-five years earlier. I thought about the enormous impact my dad had had on me by the very nature of the fact that he never acted like my dream of a flying career was something that wasn't "for girls." It was a shame she wasn't getting the same support, so I decided to change that.

I took a deep breath as I considered my options for a response. It was so hard, but I never wanted to let the kids see my disapproval of their mother. That kind of conflict wasn't in their best interest. I also felt they deserved the best possible role model, and I wanted my stepdaughter to feel the way I did, the way David had made me feel: that you could do anything you wanted if you worked hard enough.

"Well, she's wrong. I know lots of female Marines."

Her face lit up.

"Cool!" she cried. "I'm gonna go play Xbox now."

If only she knew how much Xbox she'd play as a Marine.

Seeing her face light up like that when I informed her she could be a Marine made me realize what I needed to do next. It wasn't enough that I was the best I could be at my job. It wasn't enough that I was a living, breathing example of what

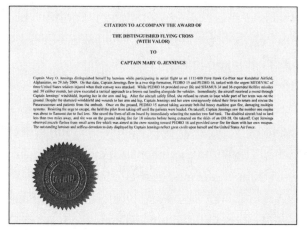

Distinguished Flying Cross (with Valor) Certification.

women were capable of. I had to find a way to contribute more to changing the conversation about this. I had lived it. I was already speaking and writing about it, but nothing had changed. Nothing *would* change unless we started fighting a little harder. Now, there was something I was good at.

———— ❂ ————

I wouldn't believe it if I'd seen it in a movie, but it's true: The timing of that conversation was meant to be, and the very next day, on July 24, 2012, I *would* get my chance to do something about it. I received a phone call from the American Civil Liberties Union from a woman named Ariela Migdal, an attorney on the Women's Rights Project team in the ACLU. They were looking into filing a lawsuit and were talking to women who had served in combat about being plaintiffs. Someone had passed my name on to them as an example of what women were capable of in combat and notified them that I had been denied the chance to compete for the job of Special Tactics Officer just because of my gender.

Without hesitation I agreed to take part in the lawsuit. I knew the case would likely cause a media frenzy, and there could be some very vocal opponents—including people I'd served with. There was a good chance my own service would be dragged through the mud as they tried to discredit me. But all I could think about was my stepdaughter's crestfallen face, how angry and confused she was when she had to confront that first taste of discrimination. I thought of my teacher in high school, Mr. Dewey, and the betrayal I'd felt when I'd realized he was making a judgment about me based solely on my gender. I had the overwhelming urge to show my daughter that you didn't have to roll over and take this kind of treatment. Even though it might get ugly, I knew I was in.

Over the next few weeks, I would meet my fellow plaintiffs and do some media training. I called my squadron in California to give them a heads-up so they wouldn't be taken by surprise when they saw the news. Mat Wenthe had taken over as commander, and I was excited for the excuse to catch up with him.

"Hey, MJ! How's Austin treating you?" he asked when I called him.

"Pretty good. You know, eating barbecue, suing the Secretary of Defense, listening to some live music . . . the usual."

"Heh, heh, yeah . . ." He stopped, realizing he wasn't getting the joke. "Wait, what?"

I took a calming breath to settle my nerves. I wasn't afraid of getting into trouble as much as I was terrified that my actions would be met with disapproval and, even worse, isolation from the men and women I had bled with in Afghanistan.

"Well, here's the deal." I laid out the lawsuit and my reasons for partnering with the ACLU on it. He didn't say a word. He just listened quietly. He finally spoke once I stopped filling the awkward silences.

"But I don't understand. Do you feel like we've ever held you back? I mean, you were right there with us in the sh*t . . . That's about as tip of the spear as you can get."

"No!" I said, realizing he wasn't about to hurt my feelings—instead it seemed like I had hurt his. "It's not you guys. This isn't about how I was treated or the policies of the unit. It's not even about air combat at all. Did you know that women are technically barred from ground combat?"

He thought about that for a second.

"Well, no . . . yeah . . . I don't know," he said. "I guess I've never really thought about it before."

Exactly. Neither had I. Why would we have? In our world, men and women were pretty seamlessly integrated already, so for most of us it wasn't a big deal.

I went on to reassure him I had felt nothing but support from the unit, but that this was something I felt strongly I had to do. He ended the conversation in typical Mat fashion.

"Well, I was roommates with the guy who won on the first season of *The Amazing Race*, so you'll be the second most famous person I know, I guess."

I smiled, a little choked up at how supportive he was being, and I started to let myself hope that the majority of the others might feel the same way. I hung up and went back to preparing for the media frenzy, nostalgic for the camaraderie of war fighters.

Just over four months after our first conversation on the phone, on November 27, 2012, we filed our suit against the Secretary of Defense under the name *Hegar, et al. v. Panetta*. The press conference we held in San Francisco that day would be the beginning of a yearslong firestorm of media attention and debate.

There were so many arguments that flared up after we lit the match, it's hard to even remember them all. Some were more ridiculous than others. One of the many arguments that ensued was over whether or not civilians (i.e., the ACLU) should be dictating such things to the military. I found this hilarious for many reasons.

First of all, the Ground Combat Exclusion Policy was a civilian-issued order in the first place. It was put in place in 1994 by then Secretary of Defense William Perry in response to the outrage over lifting the ban on females in combat cockpits. That move, so many years ago, had been met with doomsday predictions of overly emotional women ruining the Air Force with their periods, babies, and breast milk—but of course had long since been validated as the right thing to do.

Since the field has been opened to females, women have proven to be some of the best pilots in every branch. Women have been awarded medals and given command positions. They've shown resilience as prisoners of war, served as instructors, and done everything their male counterparts do without the predicted downfall of the American way of life.

Furthermore, at the most basic level, one of the things that distinguishes us from military dictatorships is that civilians have always been the ones telling the military what to do. It's one of the core elements of our history and Constitution.

The incontrovertible fact was that this current policy banning women from being in combat was not good for the military. The commanders in the field fighting the actual wars had their hands tied by this policy. Not only could women not compete for certain jobs, but the women that our commanders needed in the field could not be "assigned" to the units who faced direct ground combat. The policy was so out of touch with the actual reality on the ground that loopholes and end runs around the policy were common. Women were constantly being "attached" to these units, then rotated out after a number of days to ensure their status remained "temporary."

Women are needed on the front lines for a variety of reasons, and that's the bottom line. Either they are the best person for that particular job (say, a unit's top marksman) or they have to do a job that only a woman can do (e.g., patting down female attendees at the fragile council meetings with local warlords). Whatever the reason, women were needed on the front lines, and commanders were constantly having to tap-dance to get them out there.

One of the things that builds a team up and prepares them for the rigors of war is the training they experience together. The years I flew with my crew, the training we had all attended, solidified us as a team. We faced the same training standards and the same challenges, which created a bond that enabled us to implicitly trust one another with our lives, to depend on the person sitting next to us to watch our back when the sh*t hit the fan. The way things were set up for the ground forces, these women were being "attached" without the benefit of joint training or the chance to earn the trust of their comrades. They were almost being set up to fail, despite the fact that people on the front lines so desperately needed them to succeed.

The suit wasn't designed to force anything on the military. It was designed to untie the hands of the commanders in order to allow them to select and train the best teams for the job at hand without regard to gender. While there are some misogynistic people left who find the idea of strong female warriors threatening, the reality is that this change is supported by the vast majority of the people actually fighting the wars.

The decision makers on the front lines who have served with women in this capacity and seen what they can do want this change. Of the people opposed to this move inside the military, I have yet to meet one who has had any actual experience serving with women. For the most part, their experience is limited to imagining their sister or spouse at war, many of whom are not suited for the battlefield and probably have little in common with the women who have spent years of their lives training for combat.

In my experience, changing the minds of people whose opinions aren't based on actual facts tends to be the hardest because their beliefs are rooted in their prejudices as opposed to reality. For some people, it didn't matter what facts were presented or what accomplishments women achieved. Nothing would ever make them budge from their stubborn position. So I knew we had to be prepared to settle in for a long, hard-fought battle.

But on the morning of January 24, 2013, I was at the office when I received a surprise phone call from Mat Wenthe, my squadron commander who had been so supportive about the lawsuit. I was working at my desk, trying to keep my voice down so as not to disturb the others in the cubicle maze around me.

"Congratulations, MJ!" he exclaimed.

"On what?" I whispered as I continued my work. I had no idea what he was talking about.

"You did it!" he shouted in my ear.

Then he informed me that Secretary Panetta had just lifted the unconstitutional policy in a historic press conference with his Joint Chiefs of Staff. He did this, in part, due to our suit. But the most gratifying thing about this event was that he also did this in response to a unanimous request signed by all of his Joint Chiefs. Word had filtered up from the front lines, and the brass had heard their commanders loud and clear. The policy was bad for our military and was hurting our war efforts. Period. This wasn't about political correctness. It was well past time to rescind it.

"WOO-HOOOO!" I jumped up and yelled. Little office-worker gopher heads popped up all around me with their mouths open.

"That's awesome!" I cried.

Mat couldn't believe I didn't know it already, but he was happy to be the one to deliver the news. We would still have an uphill battle ensuring no one else put the discriminatory policy back into practice, but this was an enormous first step.

Before rescinding the policy, the default was that combat jobs were closed to women. You had to obtain an exception to get one to open. Now, by default, everything was suddenly open. With the policy lifted, the Secretary gave the branches three years to study which jobs, if any, would remain closed. Each branch would have to show substantial evidence and submit specific requests if they wanted to keep any jobs closed. All of a sudden, women all over the country had thousands of jobs open to them that, for years, they had been barred from even considering.

———— • ————

My elation over our progress was short-lived, though, as I began to hear politicians threaten to legislate the restrictions back into place. I hoped it was bravado for their constituents, but I couldn't afford to take that chance. We had come too far. I knew it would be my job to impact the national conversation and get in front of the politicians somehow.

One of my friends who had also been making great strides toward opening up combat jobs for women asked me if I would join up with her and a few others on founding an organization called the Combat Integration Initiative that was based in Washington, DC. I jumped at the chance to work with her, and together we partnered with the well-established organization Women in International Security to work to ensure that our nation's leaders didn't take a step backward and that our military leaders were required to order full integration with no exceptions.

There were so many people doing so much great work, and I was thrilled to be a drop in the bucket of progress. I took several trips out to DC from Austin, and I spoke on panels all across the country alongside people like Shoshana Johnson (America's first female African American POW) and Colonel Martha McSally (one of the first female fighter pilots and the first woman to command a fighter squadron in combat, now a representative from Arizona). I was honored and humbled by the men and women I met, worked, and collaborated with on this historic wave of change sweeping through our military. I met people from the United Nations who spoke about Security Council resolutions calling for more women in militaries around the world, citing the science behind the impact they have on peacekeeping missions and adherence to the laws of armed conflict. It was an exciting time, and I was elated to be contributing.

On June 26, 2013, I arranged a "Storm the Hill" day. It took several weeks to organize, but we pulled it off. A dozen or so of the women of the Combat Integration Initiative spent a full day meeting with congressmen and women, senators, and the staffers of the House and Senate Armed Services Committees. Some of the meetings that day got a little heated as we discussed the finer points at the root of the controversy.

MJ on MSNBC.

During one of the meetings that day, an older representative mentioned that he was concerned that the already high rate of military sexual assault would rise. I thought back to my own attack at the hands of Dr. Adams. This politician had no idea what he was talking about. It wasn't about how many women we put in combat. Men and women were being assaulted regardless of where they were stationed. I was pissed at this absurd line of inquiry and decided to go full shock and awe on him.

"Have you ever sexually assaulted anyone?" I asked him.

"No, of course not!" he spat out, completely flustered.

"Is that because you've never had the opportunity? You've never been alone with a woman in an isolated area?" I asked.

"No, of course that's not why," he replied, clearly unhappy with the direction this was heading.

"Exactly," I replied. "You've never done that because you haven't grown up in a culture where it's acceptable and even condoned to treat women—or other men, for that matter—as items issued for your exploitation. You haven't been taught that you can do whatever you want." I paused, wondering whether I should go on. *Now or never*, I thought.

"It's not acceptable in civilized society to treat people that way, and that's the problem the military is facing. It's not a problem of keeping potential victims from being alone and isolated with potential predators, but reversing the predator *culture* that currently exists."

I stopped, sensing he had no desire to issue a rebuttal. There are people who think that this culture is fine, given the ugly nature of war. But I and so many of my fellow servicemen and servicewomen had *proven* that you could be a tough combat warrior without being a sociopath.

Male, female, it didn't matter. We were cogs in a machine, ordered not to speak up or talk back, and the result of that, unfortunately, can be tragic for the individuals involved.

The representative, wisely, seemed to either find that answer acceptable or he didn't want to risk another similar exchange, so he moved on to his next concern. I nodded as I listened intently, giving no indication that the conversation and the memory of my own attack had rattled me a bit. I took a deep breath to address his next question and pushed the bile down back into my stomach. This was way too important to too many people for me to throw in the towel now.

All in all, the time I spent in DC and on television and radio shows was well worth the difficult moments. I finally felt like I was making a dent when I watched as senators started using the talking points that I had crafted and proliferated out into the media. I was honored to represent the women fighting and bleeding on our battlefields. Having my name appear on lists like *Newsweek* magazine's 125 Women of Impact for 2012 and *Foreign Policy* magazine's 100 Leading Global Thinkers of 2013 was absolutely surreal. To be included in the ranks of people like Malala Yousafzai and Pope Francis was more of a nod to the great strides female soldiers were making than it was personal recognition. I took every opportunity I could to speak to the world about the great things these women were doing.

Being so outspoken on such a controversial topic is not without its cost, though, and this particular topic seems to bring out the worst in people whose fragile grasp on their idea of gender roles cannot withstand the challenge of intellectual debate. While waiting in the coat check line during *Foreign Policy* magazine's Leading Global Thinkers celebratory dinner in Washington, DC, an older gentleman behind me struck up a conversation by asking me how I was involved with the event. When I told him that I was one of the recipients and why, he began trying to convince me why women have no place in combat.

"Little lady, why can't you just leave the fightin' to the men who are so good at it? I mean, what could you possibly have to contribute?" he asked.

I grinned at the irony as I thought about all of the things

I had seen and done. We were living in a different world from the one in which this former ambassador and US Marine had served. And out of respect for his generation and his service, I attempted to politely end the conversation as I retrieved my coat. My husband, Brandon, had just emerged from the restroom and joined me, but quickly noticed the look on my face.

"Hey, what's up?" he asked with a concerned look on his face.

"Oh, nothing. This gentleman is explaining to me why women shouldn't be in combat," I said, smiling up at my sweet, supportive husband.

With eyebrows raised, Brandon helped me with my coat. Then he turned back toward the gentleman and gave him a polite nod.

"I see. Well, good luck with that, sir," he said.

With a chuckle, we both turned to go. Unfortunately, the ambassador wasn't satisfied with that and proceeded to follow us, raising his voice and drawing glances from the other attendees gathered around the venue.

We bypassed the escalator at the other end of the hall and decided to jog up the staircase in front of us, managing to lose our pursuer. Even high heels and an evening gown can't slow down this chick when she's determined to evade the enemy.

———— • ————

Despite the occasional backlash, I'll continue to speak on this topic until people stop assuming that this debate is about whether or not to allow women into combat. Women are already fighting in combat, with or without anyone's permission, and they're doing so valiantly. What they aren't doing is being trained alongside their comrades in arms, given credit for doing the same jobs as their counterparts, given promotions to jobs overseeing combat operations, or being treated like combat veterans by people back home (even some in the Veterans Administration).

Not every man has the skill set or warrior spirit for combat. Not every woman does, either. But everyone that does have that skill set should be afforded the opportunity to compete for jobs that enable them to serve in the way their heart calls them. For some people, that calling is in music or art. Some are natural teachers. There are those who will save lives with science. I was called to be a warrior and to fly and fight for my country. I was afforded the opportunity to answer that call, and because of that, I have lived a full and beautiful life.

People will always be afraid of change. Just like when we integrated racially or opened up combat cockpits to women, there will always be those who are vocal in their opposition and their fear.

History will do what it always does, however. It will make their ignorant statements, in retrospect, seem shortsighted and discriminatory, and the women who will serve their country bravely in the jobs that are now opening up will prove them wrong. Just like we always have.

ACKNOWLEDGMENTS

═══★═══

There are two people without whom this book would not be in print. To my agent and friend, Gillian MacKenzie, who has walked this long road to publication with me, believing in me every step of the way. Janie Fransson, your notes and edits took this story to another level, and I am so grateful to you for all of your help. I'll think of you every time I order a bourbon . . . so I'll think of you a lot.

There are hundreds of people without whom I would never have had such an amazing career, both in the military and out. To the men and women I've served with who epitomize the Rescue motto of "These things we do that others may live": Your sacrifices and bravery are priceless to those on the battlefield and off. Steve, TieJie, George, Dave, Finn, Darren, BT, Rhys, Blue, Astro, Jimmy, Andy, Gibby, ▇▇▇▇, Red, Nate, Matt, Dono, Zerk, Rabbit, TK, and many others, it was the honor of my lifetime to have gone into battle with you.

Ric, my Brit Commando hero, thank you for your contribution to this work and your unwavering support. Quil Lawrence, you got me off to a great start! To Penguin Random House and Berkley Publishing Group for believing in this story enough to champion it with your teams. Greg Crouch and Conley Giles, thank you for your guidance and mentoring. Pat Muller, thanks for letting me steal your loving phrase for Jude and Daniel's dedication. To Julia Bringloe, a true warrior, you are my hero, and I am humbled anytime anyone uses our names in the same sentence. To the ACLU, we may not always agree about everything, but I will be forever grateful to you for continuing to challenge the status quo.

To my stepkids, you have shown a resiliency that I aspire to myself, and I hope that the things I do today will help create a better world for you as you grow up.

To my mom, Grace Jennings, for supporting me all of these years. Your sacrifices and strength have made all of this possible. To my sister, Elaine, thank you for being Aunt Lanie to Jude and Daniel.

To my dad, David, who inspired me to try anything without wondering first if I would succeed. To all of my friends, family, and comrades in arms who have filled my life with these stories. Thank you.

And to everyone who ever tried to convince me that I couldn't win, thank you for inspiring me to prove you wrong. Na-na na-na boo-boo.

QUESTIONS FOR DISCUSSION

1) As a soldier and a pilot, how was MJ treated differently from her male counterparts?

2) Keeping in mind the moments you thought about for question 1, how did the men around MJ often react to her being treated differently than them?

3) What were some of the ways that MJ had advantages as a woman throughout her career?

4) How did MJ use her quick thinking and training when she and her team were in danger?

5) How did MJ's family support her throughout her hardships? How did she support herself?

6) When MJ is told by the man in the coat check line that women shouldn't be in combat at the *Foreign Policy* magazine's Leading Global Thinkers dinner, what does MJ's husband do? What do you think men's roles are in the fight for gender equality?

7) On page 286, MJ says that even though people will always make ignorant, discriminatory statements, women will always prove them wrong. What are some things people have assumed

about you, regardless of gender, that you've proved them wrong about?

8) Also on page 286, MJ says that people will always be afraid of change and then shows how her own story isn't dissimilar from the fight for racial integration. What similarities are there between the fight for gender equality and racial equality? How are they different?

9) Was there anything in this book that surprised you? Why or why not?

10) What would you say to someone who said you couldn't do something because of your gender, ethnicity, race, class, etc.?

Q&A WITH MJ HEGAR

Q: What do you think you learned while you were in high school that ultimately helped you throughout your career?

A: I think the most important lesson I learned was that if I wanted to be really good at something—the best, even—it would take my commitment to practice, hard work, sacrifice, and patience. I wasn't as good at soccer as I was at other things which I had put more of myself into (like piano, tennis, flying). Sometimes I see young people in my life abandoning pursuits where success doesn't just fall in their lap. I am so grateful I learned the value of hard work.

Q: What advice would you give your teenage self or any teen who wants to become a pilot?

A: Don't be someone who follows or breaks all of the rules. I was successful in part because I followed the rules that would have closed doors (I stayed off drugs and made good choices) and I broke the rules that were holding me back. Strongly consider trusting adults who have *both* a wealth of experience and your best interests at heart versus blindly doing as you're told (or doing nothing you're told). As teenagers, sometimes we want to rebel against everything. It can be hard to figure out which adults to listen to. I can tell you this: Find role models whose judgment you have to acknowledge seems superior to other adults (whether they are successful in their lives, seem happier than the rest, etc.) and weigh their advice carefully when it conflicts with others.

Q: What do you wish you knew before deciding to become a pilot?

A: I wish I had known that the way people treated me (from kindergarten up) usually had more to say about them than it did about me. I am grateful that I did internalize enough to make me constantly striving to be better, study harder, and become stronger, but a healthy self-esteem and confidence are also keys to success. I wish I had known it was okay to ask for and accept help, whether that was therapy for post-traumatic stress or joining women's empowerment clubs. I just wanted to be thought of as no different than my male counterparts, so I didn't want any help. What I didn't realize is how much help those colleagues naturally got from a patriarchal institution in the first place. The story where I'm climbing the mountain in SERE training is a good illustration of this.

Q: What was the hardest part of flight training?

A: Not quitting. There are times when it got so hard I had to stop and ask myself if it was worth it. It's easy to say, looking back, that it was. But when you're exhausted and down on yourself, it can be tempting to "punch out" (as we say, referring to ejecting from an aircraft). For this reason, don't go down a path like this or any other challenging road (like medical school) for anyone but yourself. It's hard enough to stay the course when it's your dream. If it's someone else's plan for you, it'll be all that much harder to stick it out.

Q: Are there any aspects of your career that you didn't get to include in your book?

A: Yes! There were so many great stories of the amazing men and women I served with that didn't "inform the narrative." My one regret is that the whole of this book doesn't give credit to the vast majority of the people serving our great country in uniform who do not negatively impact a toxic culture. There were plenty of guys, for example, who didn't ascribe to the toxic masculinity. There were close friendships, fun times, and empowering experiences. I felt compelled to include the challenging stories, as they are usually the ones with the lessons. But if I had another fifteen volumes, I could tell you all about the rest. It sure was a blast! I'd do it all again in a heartbeat.

Q: You talk a lot about how many pilots and soldiers became your mentors or taught you a lot throughout your service. Were there any women who were mentors to you? If not, do you wish you had had a female mentor at some point in your career?

A: I don't want to undervalue the impact of women having female mentors and role models. And I certainly had them. However, there were vastly more men just given the nature of the demographics of both the Aircraft Maintenance and Aviation career fields. This whole thing started because I wanted to be Han Solo from *Star Wars*. I just never identified with Princess Leia. And I think that's okay! I had a manager in one of my civilian jobs who told me he was working hard to find me a mentor, but that there were so few female executives. I think it's a mistake to think that men can't be great mentors to women and vice versa. There is nothing wrong with women seeking out female mentors and role models when possible, but don't limit yourself!

Q: What would you say to other women or other-gendered people looking to join the military? What advice would you give them?

A: The same as I would give to the men: jump in! Your country needs you! In my opinion, it's very rarely a mistake to join the military. If it's not a good fit, you get out at the end of your commitment with real job experience and marketable skills. Now, it *is* a mistake to join for the wrong reasons or to completely believe your recruiter. Try hard to talk to multiple people in the branch and/or job you are pursuing. Put more weight in the advice of people who don't directly benefit from you signing up. Try *hard* to go to college first. But if that's not in the cards, work hard, be the best at whatever job you have, take advantage of any part-time schooling or certifications that will serve you well on the outside! Pick a career field that you are really passionate about or that will land you a great job after your service (like computers or communications). No matter your gender, I will also say this: When the going gets tough and you have to stand up and say something, it will go a lot better for you if you have already established some credibility. If you're always complaining, always the victim, always making it harder for others (like not carrying your weight), then even if the stand you're making is valid, you will have a hard time.

Q: What surprised you most in your career as a pilot?

A: How much different it was in the movies! There was so much work and a lot of "additional duties." It wasn't all adrenaline and glory. But I'm here to tell you it was totally worth it!

Q: Do you think the world is getting closer to true gender equality?

A: Sometimes it feels like one step forward and two steps back. Other times it seems as though we have to relitigate our civil liberties every generation. I hope that's changing given the level of engagement of younger generations as well as easier access to information. The problem is that there is also greater access to misinformation. I don't know if we are getting closer, but I do know this. Live your life to the fullest and make the biggest impact you can. That's all you can do, and that's what this whole crazy ride is about.

In closing, let me leave you with this: If I had a life motto it would be "No regrets." No "I should have tried this or that" on your deathbed. Don't settle. Don't give up. Now get out there and kick some serious butt!